# AMALFI COAST

## TRAVEL GUIDE 2025

Journey Through Italy's Mediterranean Paradise – A Curated Exploration of Its Most Stunning Towns, Culture, and Experiences"

## ALL RIGHTS RESERVED

No part of this publication By RUSSELL E. JONES may be reproduced, distributed, or transmitted in any form or by any means, including photocopying, recording, or other electronic or mechanical methods, without the prior written permission of the publisher, except in the case of brief quotations embodied in critical reviews and certain other noncommercial uses permitted by copyright law.

## DISCLAIMER

This travel guide is provided for informational purposes only. The information contained herein is believed to be accurate and reliable as of the publication date, but may be subject to change. We are not making any warranty, express or implied, with respect to the content of this guide.

Users of this guide are responsible for verifying information independently and consulting appropriate authorities and resources prior to travel. We are not liable for any loss or damage caused by the reliance on information contained in this guide.

Information regarding travel advisories, visas, health, safety, and other important considerations can change rapidly. Users are advised to check for the most up-to-date information from official government and travel industry sources before embarking on any trip.

Travel inherently involves risk, and users are responsible for making their own informed decisions and accepting any associated risks.

# TABLE OF CONTENT

**Chapter 1. Introduction to the Amalfi Coast** — 7
   1.1 Overview of the Amalfi Coast — 7
   1.2 Why Visit the Amalfi Coast in 2025? — 11
   1.3 Best Time to Visit the Amalfi Coast — 16

**Chapter 2. Getting to the Amalfi Coast** — 21
   2.1 Nearest Airports & Train Stations: How to Reach the Amalfi Coast in 2025 — 21
   2.2 Transportation Options on the Amalfi Coast: Car, Ferry, and Bus — 25
   2.3 Driving vs. Public Transport — 29

**Chapter 3. Exploring the Amalfi Coast: Towns & Villages** — 35
   3.1 Positano – The Iconic Cliffside Village — 35
   3.2 Amalfi – A Hub of History and Culture — 40
   3.3 Ravello – The Romantic Hilltop Escape — 44
   3.4 Sorrento – Gateway to the Amalfi Coast — 49

**Chapter 4. Top Attractions & Landmarks** — 55
   4.1 Path of the Gods Hike (Sentiero degli Dei) — 55
   4.2 Villa Rufolo & Villa Cimbrone – Timeless Treasures of Ravello — 58
   4.3 Cathedral of Amalfi & Paper Museum – A Journey Through Faith and Craftsmanship — 60
   4.4 Emerald Grotto & Fiordo di Furore – Nature's Hidden Wonders on the Amalfi Coast — 66
   4.5 Marina Grande & Hidden Beaches – The Amalfi Coast's Scenic Seaside Retreats — 71
   4.6 Ferriere Valley Nature Reserve – A Serene Escape into Nature — 77
   4.7 Sentiero degli Dei & Scenic Viewpoints – A Hiker's Paradise with Breathtaking Views — 81

**Chapter 5. Amalfi Coast Experiences & Activities** — 85
   5.1 Boat Tours & Coastal Cruises – A Unique Way to Discover the Amalfi Coast by Sea — 85
   5.2 Tasting & Lemon Groves – Savoring the Flavors of the Amalfi Coast — 88
   5.3 Cooking Classes & Local Markets – A Deep Dive into Amalfi's Culinary Heritage — 90

**Chapter 6. Where to Stay: Accommodation Guide** — 96
   6.1 Luxury Hotels & Resorts – Indulge in Amalfi's Finest Stays — 96
   6.2 Boutique Hotels & Villas – Intimate Charm and Unique Stays on the Amalfi Coast — 99
   6.3 Budget-Friendly Stays & B&Bs – Affordable Charm on the Amalfi Coast — 103
   6.4 Best Areas to Stay on the Amalfi Coast — 108

**Chapter 7. Food & Drink: Culinary Guide** — **115**
    6.1 Must-Try New Mexican Dishes: A Culinary Journey Through Tradition and Flavor — 115
    6.2 Boutique Hotels & Villas – Intimate Charm and Unique Stays on the Amalfi Coast — 118
    7.3 Street Food & Local Markets — 122

**Chapter 8. Travel Tips & Essentials** — **127**
    8.1 Packing Guide for the Amalfi Coast — 127
    8.2 Budgeting & Cost-Saving Tips for the Amalfi Coast — 131
    8.3 Local Customs & Etiquette — 134

**Chapter 9. Day Trips & Excursions** — **139**
    9.1 Pompeii & Mount Vesuvius: A Journey into the Past and the Power of Nature — 139
    9.2 Naples & Its Culinary Delights — 142
    9.3 Paestum & Ancient Greek Temples — 144

**Chapter 10. Practical Information** — **147**
    10.1 Safety & Health Tips — 147
    10.2 Currency, ATMs, and Payment Tips for the Amalfi Coast — 149
    10.3 Language & Communication — 151
    10.4 Sustainable & Responsible Travel — 153

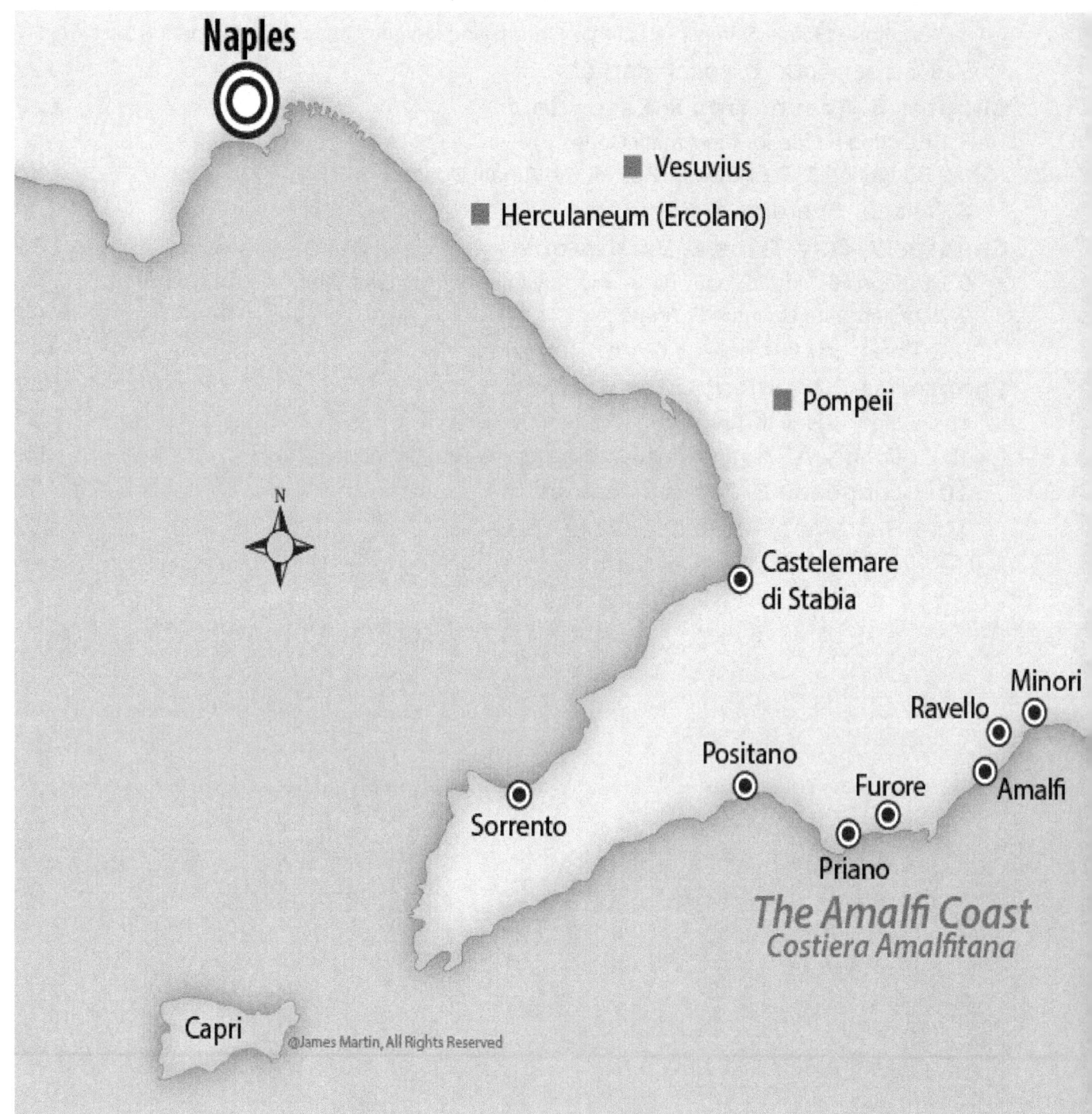

# Chapter 1. Introduction to the Amalfi Coast

## 1.1 Overview of the Amalfi Coast

The Amalfi Coast, a breathtaking stretch of southern Italy's Campania region, is an iconic destination that captivates travelers with its striking landscapes, charming villages, and rich cultural heritage. Designated as a UNESCO World Heritage Site, this 50-kilometer (31-mile) coastal paradise along the Sorrentine Peninsula boasts dramatic cliffs, turquoise waters, and a fusion of history, cuisine, and Mediterranean charm that has enchanted visitors for centuries.

A Land of Unrivaled Beauty

Renowned for its awe-inspiring scenery, the Amalfi Coast is a harmonious blend of nature and human artistry. Sheer limestone cliffs plunge into the shimmering Tyrrhenian Sea, while cascading terraces of vineyards, citrus groves, and colorful bougainvillea create a postcard-worthy panorama. The region's charming villages, each clinging to the rugged cliffs, exude a distinct character—whether it's Positano's glamorous appeal, Amalfi's historical grandeur, or Ravello's serene elegance.

The winding coastal roads offer unparalleled views at every turn, revealing quaint fishing harbors, hidden beaches, and ancient stone pathways leading to breathtaking viewpoints. This coastline is not just a place to visit but a spectacle to behold—a masterpiece of nature and tradition woven together over centuries.

A Tapestry of History and Culture

Beyond its striking beauty, the Amalfi Coast is steeped in history that dates back to antiquity. During the Middle Ages, Amalfi emerged as one of Italy's most powerful maritime republics, rivaling Venice, Pisa, and Genoa in Mediterranean trade. The remnants of this illustrious past are still evident today in the town's grand **Duomo di Sant'Andrea**, medieval watchtowers, and narrow alleyways lined with historic buildings.

Other villages have their own fascinating legacies. Ravello, once a retreat for aristocrats and wealthy merchants, boasts lavish villas and terraced gardens that continue to inspire visitors today. Positano, originally a humble fishing village, transformed into a chic resort town without losing its authentic charm. Meanwhile, Praiano, Conca dei Marini, and Maiori retain a more tranquil ambiance, providing a peaceful escape from the bustling tourist hotspots.

For centuries, the Amalfi Coast has been a muse for artists, writers, and musicians. Richard Wagner composed in Ravello, while John Steinbeck famously described Positano's dreamlike beauty. Today, this region continues to attract creatives, honeymooners, and luxury travelers seeking a haven of romance and inspiration.

Geography & Climate: A Year-Round Paradise

The Amalfi Coast's unique geography—defined by steep cliffs, deep valleys, and lush Mediterranean vegetation—creates an exceptional microclimate, making it an enticing destination in any season.

- **Spring (March–May):** One of the most picturesque times to visit, as wildflowers bloom and temperatures remain mild, with fewer crowds compared to summer.

- **Summer (June–August):** The peak season brings warm, sunny days, vibrant festivals, and a lively atmosphere, with temperatures reaching 30°C (86°F) or higher.
- **Autumn (September–November):** Still warm but with fewer tourists, offering an ideal setting for hiking, sightseeing, and enjoying local harvests, including grape and olive picking.
- **Winter (December–February):** A tranquil period with cool, crisp air and stunning, crowd-free landscapes—perfect for those who appreciate solitude and a slower pace.

The Tyrrhenian Sea moderates the climate, ensuring mild winters and pleasant summers. This makes the Amalfi Coast a dream destination for travelers at any time of year, whether they seek sun-soaked beaches, cultural exploration, or scenic hiking trails.

Traditions and Local Life: A Celebration of Heritage

Life on the Amalfi Coast is deeply rooted in tradition, and local culture is celebrated with enthusiasm through festivals, cuisine, and artisanal crafts. One of the most famous regional specialties is **Sfusato Amalfitano**, a variety of lemon grown on terraced farms along the cliffs. These lemons are used to produce **limoncello**, a sweet and aromatic liqueur that embodies the essence of the Amalfi Coast.

Throughout the year, various festivals and religious celebrations bring the towns to life. The **Luminaria di San Domenico** in Praiano illuminates the village with thousands of candles, while Easter processions in Amalfi showcase centuries-old religious traditions. Music lovers flock to Ravello for its annual **Ravello Festival**, a celebration of classical music set against the backdrop of stunning villa gardens.

Local artisans continue to preserve age-old crafts, from intricate ceramics in Vietri sul Mare to handmade sandals in Positano. These traditions add a sense of authenticity and charm, making every moment spent here feel like a step back in time.

A Destination for Every Type of Traveler

Whether you're seeking relaxation, adventure, or cultural immersion, the Amalfi Coast offers something for every kind of traveler:

- **For Nature and Outdoor Enthusiasts:**

  - Hike the legendary **Sentiero degli Dei (Path of the Gods)** for breathtaking views of the coastline.
  - Explore the **Ferriere Valley Nature Reserve**, a hidden gem filled with waterfalls and lush forests.
  - Take a boat trip to discover sea caves, secluded beaches, and the famous **Emerald Grotto**.

- **For Luxury Travelers:**

  - Stay in elegant, world-class hotels with panoramic views and infinity pools.
  - Enjoy private boat tours along the coastline, indulging in sunset aperitifs on the water.
  - Dine at **Michelin-starred restaurants**, savoring gourmet Italian cuisine with a coastal flair.

- **For History and Architecture Lovers:**

  - Visit **Amalfi's Duomo di Sant'Andrea**, an architectural masterpiece with Arab-Norman influences.
  - Wander through **Ravello's Villa Cimbrone and Villa Rufolo**, two of Italy's most enchanting estates.
  - Explore ancient **Saracen watchtowers**, remnants of the coast's defensive past.

- **For Food Lovers:**

  - Taste freshly made **scialatielli pasta** with seafood, a signature dish of the region.
  - Experience an authentic Neapolitan pizza in nearby **Sorrento**, just a short drive away.
  - Visit a **lemon grove** to learn about the production of limoncello and Amalfi's citrus heritage.

- **For Beachgoers and Relaxation Seekers:**

  - Lounge on the golden sands of **Marina Grande** in Positano or **Spiaggia del Fornillo**.
  - Escape to the secluded **Fiordo di Furore**, a dramatic fjord-like beach hidden between cliffs.
  - Unwind at luxurious beach clubs, where crystal-clear waters and refreshing cocktails await.

More Than a Destination—A Sensory Experience

The Amalfi Coast is more than just a place to visit—it is an experience that engages all the senses. The sight of pastel-hued houses clinging to cliffs, the scent of citrus groves and sea breeze, the taste of freshly caught seafood, the sound of church bells echoing through medieval streets, and the feeling of warm sun on your skin—each moment here is unforgettable.

It is a place where time slows down, where romance lingers in the air, and where every traveler finds their own slice of paradise. Whether you're admiring a sunset over Positano, wandering through centuries-old lemon groves, or sipping espresso in a charming piazza, the Amalfi Coast offers an enchanting escape unlike any other.

In this magical corner of Italy, beauty is not just seen—it is felt, lived, and cherished.

## 1.2 Why Visit the Amalfi Coast in 2025?

The Amalfi Coast has long been one of Italy's most beloved destinations, captivating travelers with its dramatic cliffs, charming seaside villages, and rich cultural heritage. While it remains an iconic location year after year,

2025 offers a particularly special opportunity to experience this breathtaking region in an even more rewarding way. Whether you're visiting for the first time or returning to relive its magic, 2025 presents a perfect blend of cultural revival, sustainability, exclusive experiences, and new attractions that make it an ideal time to explore the Amalfi Coast.

1. A Cultural Renaissance: The Return of Traditional Festivals and Events

After years of fluctuating tourism, 2025 marks a vibrant revival of local traditions, with historic festivals and cultural events returning to their full grandeur. This year promises an authentic and immersive experience of Amalfitan life, as age-old celebrations, processions, and artistic performances take center stage once again.

Must-See Festivals in 2025:

- **Regatta of the Ancient Maritime Republics (Regata delle Antiche Repubbliche Marinare) – Amalfi (June 2025)**
  Step back in time as Amalfi commemorates its maritime legacy in this spectacular boat race against Pisa, Genoa, and Venice. Expect a grand procession of medieval costumes, historical reenactments, and thrilling rowing competitions along the coastline.

- **Festival of Sant'Andrea – Amalfi (June & November 2025)**
  Honoring Amalfi's patron saint, St. Andrew, this festival blends religious devotion with festive celebrations, including awe-inspiring processions, lively street performances, and dazzling fireworks over the sea.

- **Ravello Festival (July–September 2025)**
  One of Italy's most prestigious music and arts festivals, held in the stunning gardens of Villa Rufolo. In 2025, world-class orchestras, opera performances, and contemporary art exhibitions will take center stage in this magical clifftop setting.

- **Luminaria di San Domenico – Praiano (August 2025)**
  A mesmerizing festival where thousands of candles illuminate the town, creating an enchanting, fairy-tale-like atmosphere. This event, honoring Saint Dominic, is a dream for photographers and romantics

alike.

Visiting in 2025 allows travelers to experience these vibrant traditions firsthand, offering a deeper connection to the region's cultural heritage and the warmth of its people.

## 2. A More Sustainable & Exclusive Travel Experience

### Commitment to Sustainable Tourism

With increasing efforts to preserve the Amalfi Coast's natural beauty and cultural authenticity, 2025 brings enhanced sustainability initiatives aimed at responsible tourism. Authorities have implemented measures to balance visitor numbers with environmental conservation, ensuring a more enjoyable and mindful experience for all.

Key sustainability efforts include:
- ✔ **Limited access to overcrowded areas**, protecting the integrity of historic sites and landscapes.
- ✔ **Eco-friendly transportation**, featuring electric buses and expanded ferry routes to reduce road congestion.
- ✔ **Green hospitality initiatives**, with hotels and restaurants embracing organic produce, local sourcing, and waste reduction.

By traveling in 2025, visitors contribute to these sustainable efforts, helping protect the region while still enjoying its wonders.

### New Crowd-Control Policies for a More Relaxing Visit

Overcrowding in peak seasons has been a challenge in previous years, particularly in hotspots like Positano and Amalfi. However, 2025 introduces improved crowd-management strategies to create a more intimate and stress-free travel experience.

- ✔ **Timed entry reservations** for popular sites such as the Path of the Gods and the Emerald Grotto.
- ✔ **Expanded pedestrian-only zones** in high-traffic villages, allowing for a more relaxed and immersive atmosphere.
- ✔ **Enhanced ferry schedules**, making coastal travel smoother and reducing reliance on car transportation.

These improvements ensure that visitors in 2025 will enjoy a more serene, authentic version of the Amalfi Coast—without the overwhelming crowds of past peak seasons.

3. Exciting New & Restored Attractions in 2025

A new wave of cultural and historical restoration projects makes 2025 an exciting year for discovery on the Amalfi Coast.

Newly Opened & Restored Sites to Explore:

- **Torre Trasita – Positano** (Newly Opened in 2025)
  A medieval watchtower once used to defend against pirate invasions, Torre Trasita has been fully restored and now offers breathtaking panoramic views over Positano's coastline.

- **The Expanded Amalfi Maritime Museum**
  A major renovation has transformed Amalfi's historic museum into a state-of-the-art exhibition space, showcasing rare artifacts, interactive displays, and multimedia presentations on the region's seafaring past.

- **New Hiking Trails & Viewpoints**
  Several off-the-beaten-path trails have been revitalized for 2025, offering fresh perspectives on the coastline. These include new panoramic viewpoints along the famous **Path of the Gods**, as well as the **Monte Tre Calli hike**, a lesser-known gem for adventure seekers.

4. A Culinary Renaissance: The Food Scene Reimagined

The Amalfi Coast's world-renowned cuisine is reaching new heights in 2025, as local chefs and restaurants innovate while staying true to traditional flavors. Farm-to-table dining, organic experiences, and Michelin-starred creativity define the region's latest food scene.

Must-Try Culinary Experiences in 2025:

- **Revamped Limoncello Tours:**
  Eco-friendly lemon farms now offer hands-on experiences where visitors can harvest lemons and craft their own limoncello while

- **Michelin-Starred Dining Evolves:**
  Several acclaimed chefs are introducing bold new takes on classic dishes, with freshly awarded Michelin-starred restaurants in **Positano and Ravello** leading the charge.

- **Gastronomic Tours & Cooking Classes:**
  Explore **clifftop vineyards in Furore**, join immersive cooking classes with local chefs, and embark on guided food tours to sample regional delicacies straight from local markets.

Food lovers visiting in 2025 will experience an exquisite balance of authenticity and innovation, making the Amalfi Coast a true paradise for culinary exploration.

5. More Affordable & Flexible Travel Options

While the Amalfi Coast is known for luxury, 2025 brings new opportunities for budget-conscious travelers without sacrificing quality.

✔ **New Boutique Hotels & B&Bs:** A wave of stylish yet affordable accommodations has opened, offering charming stays at a fraction of the price.
✔ **Flexible Flight & Train Discounts:** Special promotions from airlines and rail companies make reaching Naples and Salerno more affordable than ever.
✔ **Off-Peak Travel Deals:** March–April and October–November 2025 offer lower prices, pleasant weather, and fewer tourists—making for an ideal time to visit.

6. A Once-in-a-Lifetime Opportunity to Experience a Timeless Destination

While the Amalfi Coast is always a dream destination, 2025 stands out as a particularly remarkable year to visit. With its revival of cultural traditions, enhanced sustainability measures, newly restored attractions, and an evolving culinary scene, the coastline is more enchanting than ever.

Whether you seek adventure on scenic trails, sun-soaked relaxation on idyllic beaches, historical exploration through ancient towns, or indulgence in world-class cuisine, 2025 presents a rare opportunity to experience the Amalfi Coast at its best.

With fewer crowds, improved infrastructure, and a vibrant cultural scene, this is the perfect year to turn your Italian dream trip into reality—an unforgettable journey through one of the most breathtaking destinations in the world.

## 1.3 Best Time to Visit the Amalfi Coast

The Amalfi Coast is a dream destination year-round, offering breathtaking landscapes, stunning Mediterranean waters, and a vibrant cultural scene. However, the experience you'll have depends greatly on when you visit. Each season brings its own advantages and challenges, from perfect beach weather in summer to quiet, crowd-free exploration in winter. In this section, we'll break down the best times to visit the Amalfi Coast in 2025, based on weather, crowds, prices, and activities.

### 1.3.1 Understanding the Amalfi Coast's Seasons

The Amalfi Coast experiences a Mediterranean climate, characterized by hot, dry summers and mild, wet winters. Here's a breakdown of what to expect in each season:

**Spring (March – May): The Best Balance of Weather, Crowds & Prices**

- Average Temperature: 15°C–24°C (59°F–75°F)
- Crowds: Moderate; growing toward late May
- Prices: Affordable in March, moderate in April, increasing in May
- Best For: Sightseeing, hiking, photography, festivals, early beach days

Spring is one of the best times to visit the Amalfi Coast, as the landscape bursts into color with blooming wildflowers, lemon trees in full blossom, and pleasantly warm temperatures that are perfect for outdoor exploration.

**Why Visit in Spring?**
✔ Comfortable Weather – Warm enough for outdoor activities without the scorching heat of summer.
✔ Ideal for Sightseeing & Hiking – Explore Path of the Gods, Ravello's gardens, and coastal villages without excessive crowds.
✔ Spring Festivals & Events – Attend traditional celebrations like Easter

Processions and Lemon Festival in Massa Lubrense.

✔ **Affordable Accommodation & Flights** – Hotels and flights remain reasonably priced until late May.

**Downsides:**

- The sea is still a bit chilly for swimming in March and early April.
- Some seasonal hotels and restaurants may still be closed in early March.

■ Best Spring Month to Visit: Mid-April to Mid-May for the best balance of weather, prices, and activities.

## Summer (June – August): Peak Season, Stunning But Crowded

- Average Temperature: 25°C–32°C (77°F–89°F)
- Crowds: Extremely high, especially in Positano and Amalfi
- Prices: At their highest; accommodations often fully booked
- Best For: Beach lovers, nightlife, festivals, boat tours

Summer is the busiest and hottest season on the Amalfi Coast, attracting visitors from all over the world. If you dream of long days under the sun, swimming in the Mediterranean, and sipping limoncello with a view, this is the time to go. However, it's also when the coastline gets the most crowded, and prices for accommodations and flights skyrocket.

### Why Visit in Summer?

✔ **Perfect Beach Weather** – The sea is at its warmest, ideal for swimming and boat tours.

✔ **Lively Atmosphere** – Towns are buzzing with nightlife, open-air concerts, and festivals.

✔ **Full Access to Attractions** – Everything is open, including ferries, restaurants, and beach clubs.

### Major Summer Festivals:

- Regatta of the Ancient Maritime Republics (June) – Amalfi
- Festival of Sant'Andrea (June & November) – Amalfi
- Ravello Festival (July–September) – Ravello
- Luminaria di San Domenico (August) – Praiano

**Downsides:**

- Overcrowding – Expect heavy crowds in Positano, Amalfi, and Ravello.
- High Prices – Hotels and flights are significantly more expensive.
- Traffic & Long Wait Times – Roads become congested, and restaurant reservations are a must.

■ Best Summer Month to Visit: Late June or early September (for slightly fewer crowds).

## Autumn (September – November): The Golden Season

- Average Temperature: 18°C–27°C (64°F–81°F)
- Crowds: Decreasing in October, minimal by November
- Prices: Moderate in September, cheaper in October–November
- Best For: lovers, photography, hiking, cultural experiences

Autumn is often considered the best-kept secret for visiting the Amalfi Coast. As summer crowds begin to leave, the coastline retains its warmth, making it perfect for a peaceful yet sunny getaway.

### Why Visit in Autumn?

✔ Mild Weather & Warm Sea – September still offers great swimming conditions.
✔ Perfect for Food & Lovers – Autumn is harvest season, with fresh truffles, festivals, and local delicacies.
✔ Ideal for Hiking & Exploring – Cooler temperatures make trails like Sentiero degli Dei (Path of the Gods) more enjoyable.
✔ Lower Prices & Fewer Crowds – Flights and hotels become more affordable, especially in late October.

### Notable Autumn Festivals:

- Grape Harvest Season (September–October) – Furore & Tramonti
- San Gennaro Festival (September) – Praiano

### Downsides:

- By November, some beach clubs and restaurants start closing for the season.
- Shorter daylight hours in late autumn.

■ Best Autumn Month to Visit: Mid-September to mid-October (for warm weather, fewer crowds, and affordable prices).

**Winter (December – February): The Quiet, Off-Season Escape**

- Average Temperature: 8°C–14°C (46°F–57°F)
- Crowds: Very low; mostly locals
- Prices: Lowest of the year; great for budget travelers
- Best For: Quiet retreats, photography, cultural immersion

Winter is the least popular time to visit, but it has its own charm. The Amalfi Coast transforms into a peaceful retreat, perfect for those who prefer a slower, more intimate experience.

**Why Visit in Winter?**
✔ No Crowds – Walk through Positano, Ravello, and Amalfi with barely any tourists.
✔ Cheapest Prices – Hotels and flights are at their lowest, making it ideal for budget travelers.
✔ Authentic Local Experience – Enjoy a more relaxed, traditional Amalfi without the tourist hustle.
✔ Christmas Festivities – Amalfi and Positano feature beautiful holiday markets and nativity scenes.

**Downsides:**

- Many hotels and restaurants close for the season.
- Colder weather and frequent rain.
- Limited public transport schedules.

■ Best Winter Month to Visit: December (for Christmas lights and festivities).

## 1.3.2 Final Verdict: When Should You Go?

| Season | Best For | Crowds | Weather | Price | Overall Rating |
|---|---|---|---|---|---|
| Spring (March–May) | Sightseeing, hiking, festivals | Moderate | Warm | Moderate | ★★★★★ |

| Season | Highlights | Crowds | Weather | Cost | Rating |
|---|---|---|---|---|---|
| Summer (June–August) | Beaches, nightlife, festivals | Very High | Hot | Expensive | ★★★ |
| Autumn (Sept–Nov) | , photography, fewer crowds | Moderate | Warm/Cool | Moderate | ★★★★★ |
| Winter (Dec–Feb) | Quiet, budget travel, local culture | Very Low | Cool/Rainy | Cheapest | ★★★ |

For most travelers, spring (April-May) and autumn (September-October) offer the best combination of weather, affordability, and crowd levels. However, if you're visiting primarily for beaches and nightlife, summer may still be the best choice—just be prepared for crowds and high prices.

No matter when you visit, the Amalfi Coast in 2025 promises to be an unforgettable experience!

# Chapter 2. Getting to the Amalfi Coast

## 2.1 Nearest Airports & Train Stations: How to Reach the Amalfi Coast in 2025

Planning your journey to the Amalfi Coast requires some logistical preparation, as there are no direct international airports or major train stations within the coastal region itself. Instead, travelers must fly into a nearby airport, take a train to a major city, and then continue via ferry, bus, private transfer, or rental car to reach their final destination. By understanding the best airport and train station options, you can make your arrival as smooth and efficient as possible.

2.1.1 Nearest Airports to the Amalfi Coast

Since the Amalfi Coast lacks its own airport, visitors typically fly into one of several nearby options before continuing their journey. Choosing the right airport depends on factors like international flight availability, travel time, and personal preference.

1. Naples International Airport (NAP) – Capodichino Airport

📍 **Location:** Naples, ~60 km (37 miles) from Amalfi
✈ **Best For:** Closest and most convenient airport for reaching the Amalfi Coast

Flight Options:

- **International:** Direct flights from major European cities; seasonal flights from the U.S. and Canada.
- **Domestic:** Frequent connections to Rome, Milan, Venice, and other Italian cities.

Transport Options from Naples to the Amalfi Coast:

✔ **Train** – High-speed train to Salerno or regional train to Naples Centrale.
✔ **Bus** – Direct routes to Sorrento or Salerno.
✔ **Ferry** – Direct ferries from Naples to Amalfi, Positano, and Salerno.

✔ **Private Transfer & Taxi** – Comfortable and direct door-to-door service.
✔ **Car Rental** – Ideal for a scenic drive along the Amalfi Coast.

✔ **Pros:** The closest major airport with excellent transport connections.
✘ **Cons:** Smaller than Rome's Fiumicino Airport; fewer long-haul flight options.

2. Rome Fiumicino International Airport (FCO) – Leonardo da Vinci Airport

📍 **Location:** Rome, ~280 km (174 miles) from Amalfi
✈ **Best For:** More international flight options and efficient train connections.

Flight Options:

- **International:** One of Europe's busiest airports, with direct long-haul flights from North America, Asia, and beyond.
- **Domestic:** Frequent flights to Naples, Milan, Venice, and other Italian cities.

Transport Options from Rome to the Amalfi Coast:

✔ **Train** – Direct high-speed train from Fiumicino to Rome Termini, then onward to Naples or Salerno.
✔ **Bus** – Direct long-distance bus services to Amalfi Coast towns.
✔ **Private Transfers & Car Rentals** – Flexible options for reaching the coast.

✔ **Pros:** More international flights, fast and frequent train connections.
✘ **Cons:** Longer journey to the Amalfi Coast compared to Naples Airport.

3. Rome Ciampino Airport (CIA) – Best for Budget Travelers

📍 **Location:** Rome, ~270 km (168 miles) from Amalfi
✈ **Best For:** Budget travelers flying with Ryanair, EasyJet, and other low-cost carriers.

Flight Options:

- **International:** Primarily European low-cost flights.
- **Domestic:** Limited but available connections.

Transport Options from Ciampino to the Amalfi Coast:

✔ **Bus** – Transfer to Rome Termini, then take a train to Naples or Salerno.
✔ **Car Rental** – Direct road access for independent travelers.

✔ **Pros:** Budget-friendly flight options.
✘ **Cons:** Fewer transport connections compared to Fiumicino Airport.

4. Salerno Costa d'Amalfi Airport (QSR) – A Growing Regional Option

📍 **Location:** Salerno, ~50 km (31 miles) from Amalfi
✈ **Best For:** Travelers looking for a close airport (with expanding flight options in 2025).

Flight Options:

- **International:** Limited but growing availability.
- **Domestic:** New connections expected from Milan, Rome, and other Italian cities.

Transport Options from Salerno to the Amalfi Coast:

✔ **Train** – Regional trains from Salerno to nearby towns.
✔ **Bus** – Direct routes to Positano, Amalfi, and Ravello.
✔ **Taxis & Car Rentals** – Convenient for direct access.

✔ **Pros:** The closest airport to the Amalfi Coast.
✘ **Cons:** Limited flight options, but expansion is expected in 2025.

---

2.1.2 Nearest Train Stations to the Amalfi Coast

While the Amalfi Coast itself lacks a train station, several nearby hubs provide excellent connectivity. From these stations, travelers can continue their journey via ferry, bus, or private transfer.

1. Naples Centrale Train Station (Napoli Centrale)

🚉 **Best For:** Fastest route from Rome & northern Italy.

- **High-Speed Trains:** Frecciarossa, Frecciargento, and Italo trains connect Naples to Rome in just **1 hour**.
- **Local Trains:** The Circumvesuviana line connects Naples to Sorrento (~1 hour, slower but budget-friendly).

✔ **Connections to the Amalfi Coast:**
✔ High-speed train to **Salerno**, then ferry or bus.
✔ Bus from **Naples to Positano or Amalfi**.
✔ Private transfers for direct comfort.

✔ **Pros:** Frequent and fast high-speed trains.
✘ **Cons:** Naples station area can be crowded and hectic.

2. Salerno Train Station

▮ **Best For:** Direct access to the Amalfi Coast via ferry.

- **High-Speed Trains:** Frecciarossa & Italo (Rome to Salerno ~2 hours).
- **Regional Trains:** Connections from Naples, Milan, Florence, and Venice.

✔ **Connections to the Amalfi Coast:**
✔ **Ferries from Salerno** to Amalfi, Positano, Maiori, and Minori.
✔ **Buses to Amalfi Coast towns**.
✔ **Taxis & private transfers available**.

✔ **Pros:** Best station for direct ferry access.
✘ **Cons:** Fewer high-speed train options than Naples Centrale.

3. Sorrento Train Station

▮ **Best For:** Budget travelers using the Circumvesuviana train.

- **Train Line:** Circumvesuviana (Naples–Sorrento line).

✔ **Connections to the Amalfi Coast:**
✔ **Bus from Sorrento** to Positano, Amalfi, and Ravello.
✔ **Ferries from Sorrento** to Positano & Amalfi.

✔ **Pros:** Budget-friendly option.
✘ **Cons:** Slower train; no high-speed connections.

### 2.1.3 Best Airport & Train Station Combinations for Different Travelers

Best Way to Reach the Amalfi Coast in 2025

✔ **Best Arrival Airport:** Naples International Airport (NAP) – Closest and most convenient.
✔ **Best Train Station:** Salerno – Direct ferry access to Amalfi & Positano.
✔ **Best Ferry Route:** Salerno to Amalfi/Positano – Avoids road traffic.
✔ **Best for Flexibility:** Renting a car – Perfect for independent exploration.

No matter which route you take, reaching the Amalfi Coast is part of the adventure—with breathtaking scenery and charming coastal towns waiting to be explored!

## 2.2 Transportation Options on the Amalfi Coast: Car, Ferry, and Bus

Getting around the Amalfi Coast can be as much an adventure as the destination itself. With its dramatic cliffside roads, breathtaking ferry routes, and well-connected bus services, choosing the right mode of transportation is essential for a smooth and enjoyable experience. However, navigating this stunning but challenging region requires careful planning, as the narrow, winding roads, limited parking, and seasonal crowds can significantly impact travel times. Below, we explore the pros and cons of the three main transportation options—car, ferry, and bus—so you can decide which best suits your travel style.

### 2.2.1 Renting a Car: Freedom vs. Challenges

Should You Rent a Car on the Amalfi Coast?

Driving along the Amalfi Coast can be both exhilarating and stressful. The iconic **Strada Statale 163 (SS163),** often hailed as one of the most scenic roads in the world, winds its way along steep cliffs, offering panoramic sea views at every turn. However, its narrow lanes, sharp bends, and frequent traffic congestion make it a challenging drive, especially for those unfamiliar with Italian roads.

✔ **Best For:** Travelers who want flexibility, plan to explore less-touristy villages, or visit during off-peak seasons (spring & fall).

✘ **Not Ideal For:** Summer visitors (due to heavy traffic and limited parking), nervous drivers, or those unfamiliar with steep and winding roads.

Driving Conditions & Road Rules

- **Challenging terrain:** The SS163 is a two-lane road carved into the cliffs, featuring tight turns and dramatic drops.
- **Heavy traffic:** Expect congestion, especially between **Positano and Amalfi,** where buses, scooters, and cars compete for space.
- **Seasonal restrictions:** During peak summer months, authorities may impose **one-way traffic regulations** to ease congestion.
- **ZTL (Limited Traffic Zones):** Many towns have restricted areas where only residents can drive.

Where to Rent a Car

- **Naples International Airport (NAP):** Convenient for travelers arriving by air.
- **Salerno Train Station:** A good option for those arriving by train.
- **Sorrento:** Offers rental options for those continuing to the Amalfi Coast.

Parking: The Biggest Challenge

Parking in towns like Amalfi, Positano, and Ravello is extremely limited, expensive, and often requires advance reservations.

- **Hotel parking:** €25-€50 per day, often requiring a reservation.
- **Public parking lots:** Fill up quickly and cost €5-€10 per hour.
- **Remote parking:** In some towns, visitors must park outside and walk or take a shuttle.

✔ **Pro Tip:** If you must drive, consider **staying in Sorrento or Salerno** (where parking is easier) and using public transport for day trips along the coast.

## 2.2.2 Ferries: The Most Scenic & Relaxing Option

Why Take a Ferry?

Ferries offer one of the most enjoyable and stress-free ways to travel along the Amalfi Coast. Instead of battling traffic on the winding roads, you can sit back and take in the stunning coastline from the water. Ferries also eliminate parking hassles and provide **a unique perspective of the picturesque cliffside towns.**

✔ **Best For:** Travelers seeking a relaxing and picturesque journey without the stress of driving.

✘ **Not Ideal For:** Those on a tight schedule, as ferry services are **seasonal** and dependent on weather conditions.

Main Ferry Routes & Approximate Costs

✔ **Pro Tip: Book tickets in advance** during peak season (May-September), as ferries fill up quickly.

Where to Catch a Ferry

- **Naples (Molo Beverello Port):** High-speed ferries to Sorrento, Positano, and Amalfi.
- **Salerno (Piazza della Concordia):** Ideal for those heading directly to Amalfi or Positano.
- **Sorrento Port:** A major hub with ferries to Positano, Amalfi, and Naples.
- **Positano & Amalfi Piers:** Departures to Capri, Salerno, and Sorrento.

Ferry Companies & Online Booking

- **Travelmar:** Best for Amalfi, Positano, and Salerno routes.
- **Alilauro:** Offers Naples to Sorrento connections.
- **NLG (Navigazione Libera del Golfo):** Serves Capri, Sorrento, and Positano.

✔ **Pro Tip:** Ferries **do not operate regularly in winter (November–March),** so check schedules before planning your trip.

---

2.2.3 Buses: The Most Budget-Friendly Option

Why Take a Bus?

The **SITA bus network** is the most affordable way to travel along the Amalfi Coast, connecting all major towns. Buses run frequently and are a great option for those who don't want to rent a car or pay for ferry tickets.

✔ **Best For:** Budget-conscious travelers and those staying in smaller villages.
✘ **Not Ideal For:** Visitors who dislike crowded buses and unpredictable schedules.

Main Bus Routes & Approximate Costs

✔ **Pro Tip:** Buy tickets in advance at **Tabacchi shops** or bus stations, as you **cannot always purchase them onboard.**

Challenges of Taking the Bus

- **Overcrowding:** Buses are often packed, especially during peak hours.
- **Unpredictable schedules:** Traffic congestion can cause significant delays.
- **Narrow roads:** The winding roads can be uncomfortable for those prone to motion sickness.

✔ **Pro Tip:** Take an **early morning or late evening bus** to avoid peak-hour crowds.

---

Best Transport Option for Different Travelers

For most visitors, a **combination of ferries and buses** is the most practical and enjoyable way to explore the Amalfi Coast, offering convenience, stunning views, and affordability. However, for those staying in remote areas or traveling in the off-season, renting a car may be a viable option—just be prepared for challenging roads and limited parking.

No matter how you choose to travel, the journey itself will be an unforgettable part of your Amalfi Coast experience!

## 2.3 Driving vs. Public Transport

Choosing between driving or using public transport on the Amalfi Coast is one of the most important decisions you'll make when planning your trip. Each option offers a unique experience, with pros and cons that depend on your travel style, budget, and itinerary. While a car gives you freedom and flexibility, public transport eliminates the stress of traffic and parking. This section provides a detailed comparison of both options so you can make the best choice for your trip.

### 2.3.1 Driving on the Amalfi Coast: The Good, The Bad & The Challenging

**🚗 Pros of Driving**

✔ Freedom & Flexibility: You control your schedule, stopping whenever and wherever you like.
   ✔ Access to Off-the-Beaten-Path Villages: Explore places like Furore, Tramonti, or Conca dei Marini, which public transport often doesn't reach.
   ✔ Scenic Drives: The SS163 Amalfi Drive is one of the most stunning coastal roads in the world.
   ✔ Convenient for Families & Groups: More comfortable than cramming into a crowded bus.

**✘ Cons of Driving**

✘ Traffic Congestion: The narrow coastal road is packed with buses, cars, and scooters, leading to slow travel times.
   ✘ Limited Parking: Finding parking in Amalfi, Positano, and Ravello is extremely difficult and expensive.
   ✘ One-Way Road Restrictions: During peak months, certain roads are restricted to alternating traffic flow, meaning long waits.

✘ Driving Difficulty: The steep cliffs, hairpin turns, and aggressive local drivers can be intimidating.

✘ Rental Costs: A car rental plus parking fees (€25-€50 per day) and ZTL fines (if you accidentally enter restricted zones) can make driving very expensive.

### 2.3.2 Public Transport on the Amalfi Coast: A Practical Alternative

For those who prefer a stress-free experience, public transport is the cheaper and easier way to travel the Amalfi Coast. However, it does come with some challenges, especially during peak seasons.

### 🚌 Pros of Public Transport

✔ Budget-Friendly: Buses and ferries are far cheaper than renting a car and paying for parking.

✔ Avoids Traffic Stress: No need to worry about traffic jams, road signs, or aggressive drivers.

✔ No Parking Hassles: Parking is limited and expensive—public transport removes this problem.

✔ Eco-Friendly: Using buses and ferries reduces congestion and lowers your carbon footprint.

✔ Scenic Views: Ferries provide unmatched coastal views, while buses allow you to enjoy the landscape without focusing on the road.

### ✘ Cons of Public Transport

✘ Crowded Buses & Ferries: During peak summer months, buses are often packed beyond capacity, and ferries sell out quickly.

✘ Irregular Schedules: Buses can be unreliable, especially in heavy traffic. Ferries operate on fixed timetables, meaning less flexibility.

✘ Limited Late-Night Options: Public transport largely shuts down after 9–10 PM, making it difficult for night owls.

✘ Multiple Transfers: Depending on your starting point, you may need to switch from train to ferry or bus, adding travel time.

### 2.3.3 Driving vs. Public Transport: Detailed Comparison

| Factor | Driving | Public Transport |
| --- | --- | --- |

| | | |
|---|---|---|
| Cost | Expensive (rental, fuel, parking fees) | Affordable (bus & ferry tickets) |
| Scenery | Stunning views from car, but driver must focus on road | Unobstructed views from ferry & bus |
| Convenience | Flexible, but stressful | Less flexible, but stress-free |
| Parking | Extremely difficult & costly | No need to worry |
| Traffic | Heavy congestion, especially in peak months | Buses affected, ferries bypass traffic |
| Access | Best for hidden villages & countryside | Best for major towns like Amalfi, Positano, and Ravello |
| Best For | Confident drivers who want flexibility | Tourists who prefer a relaxed experience |

✔ Pro Tip: The best strategy is to combine both methods—use a car for exploring rural areas and public transport for main towns like Positano and Amalfi.

## 2.3.4 The Best Transport Option Based on Your Travel Style

### 🏝 If You're Staying in Positano, Amalfi, or Ravello

### Best Choice: Public Transport (Bus + Ferry)

- These towns have severe parking shortages, so a car is more of a hassle than a convenience.
- Buses and ferries efficiently connect major tourist areas.

### 🏘️ If You're Staying in a Small Village (e.g., Praiano, Furore, Minori, or Maiori)

### Best Choice: Car Rental or Private Driver

- These villages have fewer public transport options.
- If you don't want to drive, private transfers can be a good (but expensive) alternative.

### 👨‍👩‍👧 If You're Traveling with Kids or a Group

### Best Choice: Private Driver or Rental Car

- Public buses can be overcrowded, making it difficult for families with small children.
- A private driver eliminates stress while offering the flexibility of a rental car.

### 💰 If You're on a Budget

### Best Choice: Public Transport

- SITA buses and ferries are the most affordable way to travel along the Amalfi Coast.
- Buy tickets in advance to avoid last-minute stress.

### 2.3.5 The Perfect Transport Strategy: A Hybrid Approach

For most travelers, the best option is to mix and match transport methods. Here's a sample itinerary using different transport modes:

### Sample 5-Day Amalfi Coast Transport Plan

- Day 1: Naples to Sorrento (Train or Ferry) → Sorrento to Positano (Ferry)
- Day 2: Positano to Amalfi (Ferry) → Amalfi to Ravello (Bus)
- Day 3: Day Trip to Capri (Ferry from Amalfi or Positano)
- Day 4: Amalfi to Maiori & Minori (Bus) → Return to Amalfi
- Day 5: Amalfi to Salerno (Ferry) → Salerno to Naples (Train)

This hybrid approach allows you to experience the coastal beauty by ferry, avoid traffic by bus, and relax without driving stress.

**Final Verdict: Should You Drive or Take Public Transport?**

**Choose a Car If...**
✔ You want to explore small villages and countryside spots.
✔ You're traveling in off-season (April-May, September-October).
✔ You're comfortable driving on steep, winding roads.

**Choose Public Transport If...**
✔ You're staying in Positano, Amalfi, or Ravello.
✔ You're traveling in peak summer months (June-August).
✔ You want a stress-free, budget-friendly option.

Ultimately, the best travel experience on the Amalfi Coast depends on your priorities. If you're comfortable with navigating tricky roads and expensive parking, a car offers freedom. If you prefer convenience and affordability, public transport is the way to go. For most travelers, a combination of ferries, buses, and occasional taxis or rentals is the perfect way to explore this stunning coastline.

# Chapter 3. Exploring the Amalfi Coast: Towns & Villages

## 3.1 Positano – The Iconic Cliffside Village

Perched dramatically on the cliffs of the Amalfi Coast, **Positano** is the epitome of Italian coastal charm. This stunning village, with its pastel-colored buildings tumbling down towards the sparkling Tyrrhenian Sea, is a dreamlike destination that has enchanted travelers, artists, and celebrities for decades. Positano's romantic atmosphere is defined by its picturesque alleys lined with vibrant bougainvillea, breathtaking sea views, and an unmistakable Mediterranean allure. Whether you're indulging in luxury at a five-star hotel, lounging on its world-famous beaches, or savoring fresh seafood at a cliffside trattoria, **Positano embodies la dolce vita at its finest.**

## 3.1.1 A Glimpse into Positano's History

Though now a glamorous seaside retreat, **Positano was once a simple fishing village with a history stretching back to ancient times.** According to legend, the town was named after **Poseidon (Neptune),** the Greek god of the sea, who dedicated it to a nymph he adored. Throughout history, Positano evolved from a Roman settlement into a flourishing maritime hub during the Middle Ages, playing a key role in trade within the **Republic of Amalfi.**

However, the town's prosperity declined in the 19th century, forcing many locals to emigrate in search of better opportunities. For years, Positano remained a quiet, forgotten village—until the **1950s, when American writer John Steinbeck visited and famously described it in Harper's Bazaar:**

*"Positano bites deep. It is a dream place that isn't quite real when you are there and becomes beckoningly real after you have gone."*

Steinbeck's words ignited global fascination with Positano, attracting artists, writers, and Hollywood's elite. Today, it remains one of Italy's most coveted destinations, a place where history, beauty, and sophistication blend seamlessly.

---

## 3.1.2 Best Things to Do in Positano

### 🏖 Relax on Positano's Stunning Beaches

Positano's beaches are legendary, offering golden sands, crystal-clear waters, and a vibrant atmosphere.

- **Spiaggia Grande** – The heart of Positano's beach scene, this lively stretch of sand is lined with luxury hotels, beach clubs, and restaurants. Sunbeds and umbrellas can be rented for a **premium price,** but the experience is well worth it.
- **Fornillo Beach** – A more secluded and tranquil alternative, accessible via a **scenic cliffside path.** Ideal for those seeking a quieter atmosphere.

- **Arienzo Beach Club** – One of Positano's most famous private beach clubs, accessible by boat. Known for its **turquoise waters, excellent service, and luxurious ambiance.**

✔️ **Pro Tip: Beach loungers can sell out quickly in peak season—reserve in advance for the best spots!**

🛕 Visit the Church of Santa Maria Assunta

One of Positano's most recognizable landmarks, **the Church of Santa Maria Assunta** features a **majolica-tiled dome** that glistens under the Mediterranean sun. Inside, the church houses the revered **Byzantine icon of the Black Madonna,** a relic said to have been brought to Positano by 12th-century pirates.

✔️ **Pro Tip: Visit at sunset when the golden light illuminates the dome for the most magical photos.**

🛍️ Indulge in Shopping & Handmade Fashion

Positano is famous for its signature **bohemian-chic style,** inspiring the global fashion movement known as **"Moda Positano."**

- **Linen Fashion:** Light, breezy linen dresses and shirts are a staple of Positano's relaxed yet elegant look.
- **Handmade Leather Sandals:** Local artisans craft custom-made sandals on the spot, molding them perfectly to your feet.
- **Artisan Ceramics & Perfumes:** Explore charming boutiques selling **hand-painted ceramics, handcrafted jewelry, and locally made fragrances.**

✔️ **Pro Tip: Many boutiques offer international shipping—so you don't have to worry about fitting your finds in your luggage!**

🚶 Wander Through Positano's Enchanting Streets

Exploring Positano on foot is the best way to soak in its beauty. Lose yourself in its **narrow alleyways, cascading staircases, and hidden viewpoints.**

- **Via Cristoforo Colombo** – One of the most picturesque streets in Positano, offering **postcard-worthy views** of the coastline.

- **Path of the Gods (Sentiero degli Dei)** – A must-do for hiking enthusiasts, this legendary trail offers **unparalleled panoramic views** of the Amalfi Coast.

✔ **Pro Tip: Wear comfortable shoes—Positano's streets are steep and filled with stairs!**

🍅 Experience Positano's Culinary Delights

Dining in Positano is a feast for both the eyes and the taste buds. Whether you're enjoying **fresh seafood, handmade pasta, or a glass of local wine,** every meal is a celebration of Italian flavors.

- **Da Vincenzo** – A beloved spot for fresh seafood and classic Neapolitan dishes.
- **La Sponda (Le Sirenuse Hotel)** – A **Michelin-starred restaurant** with a dreamy, candlelit atmosphere.
- **Chez Black** – Famous for its **heart-shaped pizzas and delicious seafood pasta,** right on the beach.
- **Il Ritrovo** – A hidden gem nestled in the hills of Montepertuso, offering **breathtaking views and authentic local cuisine.**

✔ **Pro Tip: Reserve a table well in advance—Positano's top restaurants fill up fast, especially in peak season!**

⛵ Set Sail on a Boat Tour

Seeing Positano from the water is an experience you'll never forget. Many local companies offer boat rentals and private tours to explore **hidden coves, sea caves, and nearby islands.**

- **The Emerald Grotto (Grotta dello Smeraldo):** A mesmerizing sea cave where sunlight creates a magical emerald glow.
- **Li Galli Islands:** A small archipelago steeped in **Greek mythology, said to be home to the Sirens.**
- **Capri & the Blue Grotto:** A popular day trip from Positano, visiting one of Italy's most famous natural wonders.

✔ **Pro Tip: For a truly magical experience, book a sunset boat tour with champagne!**

## 3.1.3 Where to Stay in Positano

Whether you're seeking **five-star luxury, boutique charm, or budget-friendly comfort,** Positano offers accommodations for every traveler.

🏨 Luxury Hotels

- **Le Sirenuse** – The most iconic hotel in Positano, known for its **elegant Mediterranean design.**
- **Il San Pietro di Positano** – A secluded cliffside retreat with a **private beach and Michelin-starred dining.**
- **Villa Treville** – A former private estate turned **exclusive boutique hotel.**

🏩 Mid-Range & Boutique Stays

- **Hotel Poseidon** – A charming, family-run hotel with **panoramic terraces.**
- **Eden Roc Suites** – Offers **modern comforts with stunning sea views.**
- **Casa Buonocore** – A **stylish guesthouse** in the heart of town.

💰 Budget-Friendly Options

- **Villa Maria Antonietta** – A well-rated guesthouse with **affordable prices.**
- **Ostello Brikette** – One of the few **budget-friendly hostels in Positano.**

---

## 3.1.4 Essential Tips for Visiting Positano

✔️ **Book early** – Hotels and restaurants fill up months in advance.
✔️ **Be prepared to walk** – Positano is steep, with lots of stairs.
✔️ **Skip the car** – Parking is expensive and scarce; use ferries or buses instead.
✔️ **Visit in May, September, or early October** – You'll enjoy great

weather with fewer crowds.

✔ **Reserve dining spots ahead of time** – Popular restaurants book up quickly in summer.

**Positano isn't just a destination—it's an experience.** From its breathtaking landscapes to its rich history, incredible cuisine, and luxurious ambiance, **this cliffside paradise is one of the most unforgettable places on Earth.**

## 3.2 Amalfi – A Hub of History and Culture

Amalfi, the namesake of the Amalfi Coast, stands as a vibrant testament to Italy's rich historical and cultural legacy. Unlike its neighbor Positano—which dazzles with its striking cliffside vistas—Amalfi offers a deeper dive into a storied past, characterized by its medieval roots, bustling local life, and enduring maritime traditions. Once a formidable maritime republic that commanded significant influence in the Mediterranean, Amalfi today remains a treasure trove of art, architecture, and authentic coastal living. Visitors here can wander through centuries-old piazzas, admire seafront panoramas, and savor genuine Italian experiences that blend the old with the new.

3.2.1 A Journey Through Amalfi's Storied Past

Amalfi's history reaches back to ancient Roman times, but its true golden age began in the 9th and 10th centuries, when it emerged as a powerful maritime republic. Rivaling renowned centers like Venice, Pisa, and Genoa, Amalfi was once the beating heart of Mediterranean commerce and naval prowess.

The Golden Age of the Amalfi Republic (9th–12th Century)
During its peak, Amalfi thrived as an independent state, dominating trade routes that connected Italy with North Africa and the Byzantine Empire. Its enterprising merchants were pioneers—introducing innovations such as the compass, Arabic numerals, and paper-making techniques to Europe. The creation of the Tabula Amalphitana, one of the earliest maritime legal codes, underscored the city's role in regulating trade and commerce throughout the Mediterranean. Under the leadership of figures like Duke Mansone I, the republic reached unparalleled heights before the arrival of Norman conquerors in 1131.

Decline and Resurgence
Following the Norman conquest, and later under Sicilian and Aragonese rule, Amalfi's fortunes waned. In 1343, a catastrophic tsunami devastated much of the lower town and its bustling harbor. Yet, the resilient spirit of the Amalfitani people prevailed; Amalfi gradually reemerged as a center of art, religion, and trade. Today, the town is a UNESCO World Heritage Site, where its historical landmarks and vibrant local traditions continue to celebrate its illustrious past.

3.2.2 Unmissable Experiences in Amalfi

Visit the Duomo di Amalfi (Cathedral of St. Andrew)
Dominating the central Piazza del Duomo, the Cathedral of St. Andrew is Amalfi's most imposing architectural gem. The church's design is a stunning fusion of Arab-Norman, Byzantine, and Baroque influences, best exemplified by its striking 13th-century bronze door, imported from Constantinople. Inside, the crypt houses sacred relics of St. Andrew—the town's patron

saint—adding a layer of spiritual depth to the experience. Adjacent to the cathedral, the Cloister of Paradise offers a serene escape, with its beautifully preserved 13th-century courtyard featuring Moorish arches and sweeping views over the lively piazza.

Explore the Amalfi Paper Museum (Museo della Carta)
Long before modern printing, Amalfi was renowned for its handmade paper. The Museo della Carta brings this ancient tradition to life, offering a glimpse into the historical techniques of paper-making that flourished during the Middle Ages and Renaissance. Visitors can tour a 13th-century paper mill, witness traditional production methods, and even purchase exquisite, handcrafted paper as a memorable souvenir.

Stroll Through Amalfi's Enchanting Streets
Meandering through Amalfi's narrow, winding streets is like stepping back in time. Via Lorenzo d'Amalfi, the main shopping avenue, is lined with artisan boutiques where you can find local ceramics, handcrafted limoncello, and authentic Amalfi paper. Enjoy a leisurely coffee at one of the charming outdoor cafés in Piazza del Duomo, where the ambiance reflects centuries of cultural exchange. Hidden alleys and ancient arches scattered throughout the town reveal the deep historical roots of this coastal jewel.

Taste the Legendary Amalfi Lemons and Limoncello
The region is famed for its "Sfusato Amalfitano" lemons, celebrated for their size and intense fragrance. A visit to a local lemon grove, such as Agriturismo Il Giardino di Vigliano, provides an immersive experience where you can learn about the cultivation of these iconic fruits. Sample the region's signature limoncello—a sweet, zesty liqueur made using traditional recipes—and savor lemon-infused delicacies like delizia al limone or a refreshing lemon granita.

Embark on a Boat Tour to the Emerald Grotto (Grotta dello Smeraldo)
For a truly magical experience, take a boat tour to the Emerald Grotto, a stunning sea cave renowned for its glowing, emerald-green waters. As sunlight filters through an underwater opening, the cave is bathed in a mystical light. Within its depths, visitors may glimpse the submerged remains of a Nativity scene—a hauntingly beautiful tableau that adds to the grotto's allure. Accessible by boat from Amalfi's harbor or via a short drive followed by an elevator ride, the grotto is a must-see natural wonder.

### 3.2.3 Where to Stay in Amalfi

Luxury Accommodations

For those seeking unparalleled comfort, luxury hotels such as Hotel Santa Caterina, NH Collection Grand Hotel Convento di Amalfi, and Anantara Convento di Amalfi Grand Hotel offer opulent rooms, breathtaking sea views, and exclusive services that epitomize refined coastal living.

Mid-Range and Boutique Options

Mid-range options like Hotel Marina Riviera, Residenza Luce, and Albergo L'Antico Convitto provide a blend of modern amenities and historical charm, perfect for travelers who want to experience authentic Italian hospitality without the high price tag.

Budget-Friendly Stays

For budget travelers, options like Hotel Amalfi and La Valle Delle Ferriere offer central locations and cozy accommodations at more affordable rates, ensuring you can experience Amalfi's magic without breaking the bank.

### 3.2.4 Essential Tips for Visiting Amalfi

- Visit Early or Late: To avoid the throngs of day-trippers, plan your visits to major attractions during the early morning or later in the afternoon.
- Wear Comfortable Shoes: The steep, narrow streets and numerous staircases call for sturdy, comfortable footwear.
- Opt for Ferries: Given the narrow, congested roads and limited parking, using the ferry is often the best way to arrive and move around.
- Savor Local Specialties: Don't miss out on local culinary delights, such as Scialatielli ai Frutti di Mare, and the region's famed limoncello.
- Explore Beyond the Town: Venture out to nearby areas like the Valle delle Ferriere, a lush nature reserve with waterfalls and ancient ruins, for a more expansive view of the region's natural beauty.

Summary

Amalfi is far more than just a stunning coastal town; it is a living chronicle of Italian maritime history, cultural evolution, and artistic brilliance. From the majestic Duomo di Amalfi and the historical Amalfi Paper Museum to the delightful local markets and the legendary lemons that define the region, every corner of Amalfi tells a story. Whether you're wandering its ancient streets, enjoying a boat ride to a glowing grotto, or simply savoring the local cuisine, Amalfi offers a rich tapestry of experiences that encapsulate the very essence of the Amalfi Coast. This enchanting destination invites travelers to immerse themselves in its history, indulge in its flavors, and create memories that will last a lifetime.

## 3.3 Ravello – The Romantic Hilltop Escape

Perched high above the Amalfi Coast, Ravello is a place of dreamy landscapes, refined elegance, and artistic inspiration. Unlike its coastal counterparts, this hilltop town is known for its serene atmosphere, breathtaking vistas, and rich cultural heritage. Often called the "City of Music", Ravello has enchanted writers, poets, and musicians for centuries, drawing visitors who seek peace, romance, and unparalleled beauty away from the bustling seaside towns.

Ravello's charm lies in its historic villas, stunning gardens, and dramatic clifftop views over the Tyrrhenian Sea. With its luxurious ambiance, world-class music festivals, and architectural splendor, Ravello offers a unique and intimate experience of the Amalfi Coast. Whether you're wandering through its medieval streets, exploring historic estates, or soaking in the panoramic views, Ravello feels like a fairytale destination suspended between the sky and sea.

### 3.3.1 A Glimpse into Ravello's History

Ravello's origins trace back to the 9th century, when it was founded as a refuge for noble families fleeing Lombard and Saracen invasions. It quickly became a thriving commercial and cultural center, especially during the 11th and 12th centuries, when it was a major part of the Maritime Republic of Amalfi.

## ♛ The Rise & Prosperity of Ravello (11th-13th Century)

- Ravello flourished as an aristocratic hub, attracting wealthy merchants and influential families.
- It became famous for its fine wool production, known as "Celendra," which was exported to markets across Italy and Byzantium.
- The town's elite built magnificent palaces and gardens, many of which still stand today.
- Ravello developed a strong cultural identity, attracting scholars, poets, and artists during the Middle Ages.

## ⚔ Decline & Cultural Renaissance

- By the 14th century, Ravello's power diminished due to political shifts and economic decline.
- However, it remained a sanctuary for artists, musicians, and intellectuals, gaining international fame in the 19th and 20th centuries.
- Notable figures like Richard Wagner, Virginia Woolf, and Gore Vidal found inspiration in its landscapes.

- Today, Ravello is a prestigious cultural destination, known for its music festivals, historic sites, and romantic atmosphere.

### 3.3.2 Best Things to Do in Ravello

### 🏛 Visit Villa Rufolo – A Timeless Masterpiece

Villa Rufolo is one of Ravello's most iconic landmarks, a historic medieval villa that blends Arab, Norman, and Gothic influences.

- Built in the 13th century by the powerful Rufolo family, the villa was once one of the grandest estates on the Amalfi Coast.
- The gardens offer spectacular sea views, famously inspiring Richard Wagner's opera "Parsifal" in 1880.
- The Ravello Festival (July-September) hosts world-renowned concerts in the villa's stunning gardens.
- Explore the ancient towers, courtyards, and frescoed halls, which exude an air of medieval grandeur.

### 🌿 Stroll Through Villa Cimbrone – The Most Romantic Spot in Ravello

Villa Cimbrone is a magnificent 11th-century estate, transformed into one of the most breathtaking gardens in Italy.

- The "Terrace of Infinity" (Terrazza dell'Infinito) is the highlight, offering uninterrupted panoramic views over the Amalfi Coast.
- Marvel at the classical statues, rose gardens, and hidden pathways, which create a truly magical setting.
- The villa was frequented by luminaries like Virginia Woolf, Winston Churchill, and Greta Garbo, cementing its reputation as a romantic retreat.
- Today, Villa Cimbrone houses a luxury hotel, though its gardens remain open to the public.

### 🎶 Experience the Ravello Festival – The Amalfi Coast's Musical Heartbeat

The Ravello Festival is one of Italy's most prestigious classical music festivals, held annually from July to September.

- Originating in 1953, it was inspired by Richard Wagner's visit to Ravello.
- Concerts take place in Villa Rufolo's gardens, with an enchanting sea-view stage suspended over the cliffs.
- The festival features orchestral performances, ballet, jazz, and chamber music, attracting top international musicians.
- Attending a concert here is a once-in-a-lifetime experience, combining world-class music with breathtaking scenery.

### 🏰 Explore the Ravello Cathedral (Duomo di Ravello)

Ravello's Duomo (Cathedral of San Pantaleone) is a stunning example of Romanesque architecture, dating back to 1086.

- The cathedral features a striking bronze door, made in Constantinople in the 12th century.
- Inside, the marble pulpit, supported by intricately carved lions, is an artistic masterpiece.
- The Chapel of San Pantaleone houses a vial of the saint's blood, which is said to liquefy annually on his feast day (July 27th).

### 🍽 Indulge in Fine Dining with a View

Ravello is home to some of the Amalfi Coast's finest restaurants, where Mediterranean flavors meet Michelin-star quality.

- Rossellinis – A Michelin-starred restaurant offering exquisite Italian cuisine with a stunning panoramic terrace.
- Belmond Hotel Caruso's Restaurant – A luxurious dining experience with breathtaking views and gourmet dishes.
- Ristorante Raffaele – A hidden gem offering fresh seafood and traditional Campanian dishes in a relaxed setting.

## 3.3.3 Best Places to Stay in Ravello

### 🏨 Luxury Hotels

- Belmond Hotel Caruso – A 5-star palace hotel with a famous infinity pool overlooking the coastline.
- Palazzo Avino – A historic pink-hued mansion turned into a luxury retreat with sea-view terraces.
- Villa Cimbrone Hotel – A secluded and elegant stay within one of Italy's most famous gardens.

## 🌲 Mid-Range & Boutique Stays

- Hotel Rufolo – A charming hotel with medieval architecture and garden views.
- Villa Maria – A boutique hotel with organic cuisine and stunning terrace views.
- La Moresca – A stylish family-run guesthouse with a rooftop terrace and romantic ambiance.

## 🏠 Budget-Friendly Options

- B&B Ravello Rooms – A cozy stay with affordable prices and great views.

- Al Borgo Torello – A charming B&B nestled in the hills, offering an authentic Ravello experience.

### 3.3.4 Tips for Visiting Ravello

✔ Visit in the Morning or Late Afternoon – The afternoons get crowded, especially during peak season.
✔ Wear Comfortable Shoes – Ravello's streets are steep and uneven, so be prepared for walking.
✔ Plan Your Visit Around the Ravello Festival – If you love classical music, experiencing a concert under the stars is unforgettable.
✔ Stay Overnight for a Romantic Experience – While many visit Ravello as a day trip, an overnight stay offers a magical, tranquil ambiance after sunset.
✔ Explore Beyond the Main Sites – Walk the Sentiero dei Limoni (Path of Lemons), a scenic trail connecting Ravello to Minori.

Ravello is the crown jewel of the Amalfi Coast, a place of romance, culture, and breathtaking beauty. Whether you're exploring historic villas, attending world-class concerts, or simply gazing at the endless sea views, Ravello offers an experience that feels almost otherworldly. It's a town where art, history, and nature blend seamlessly, making it a must-visit destination for travelers seeking elegance, inspiration, and tranquility.

## 3.4 Sorrento – Gateway to the Amalfi Coast

Sitting at the northern edge of the Sorrentine Peninsula, Sorrento is often considered the gateway to the Amalfi Coast. With its dramatic cliffs, vibrant piazzas, rich history, and breathtaking sea views, Sorrento is more than just a transit hub—it is a destination in its own right. Overlooking the Bay of Naples, with Mount Vesuvius as a backdrop, this coastal town has long been a favorite retreat for travelers, poets, and artists.

Famed for its lemons, Limoncello, historic architecture, and relaxed Mediterranean charm, Sorrento offers a unique blend of Italian elegance and coastal beauty. It is well connected to Naples, Capri, and the Amalfi Coast, making it a strategic base for exploring the region. Whether you're wandering through narrow cobblestone streets, sipping Limoncello at a seaside café, or admiring the stunning views from Villa Comunale Park, Sorrento captures the essence of southern Italy's dolce vita.

**3.4.1 A Glimpse into Sorrento's History**

Sorrento has a history that stretches back to ancient times, with origins rooted in Greek and Roman civilizations. The town has seen the rise and fall of empires, the influx of traders, and the inspiration of artists who sought to capture its beauty.

### 🏺 Ancient Sorrento: Greek & Roman Influence

- The Greeks first settled in Sorrento around the 8th century BC, laying the foundation for its strategic coastal position.
- The Romans later took control in 4th century BC, transforming it into a popular retreat for aristocrats who built lavish villas along the cliffs.
- Remnants of Roman villas and baths can still be found along the coast, with sites like the Villa di Pollio Felice at Capo di Sorrento.

### 👑 Medieval & Renaissance Period

- During the Middle Ages, Sorrento became an independent duchy, frequently attacked by Saracen pirates.
- The town built defensive walls and fortifications, some of which still exist today.

- By the 18th and 19th centuries, Sorrento became a stop on the Grand Tour, attracting European intellectuals, including Lord Byron, Charles Dickens, and Goethe.

### 🌙 Sorrento Today

- Today, Sorrento is a cosmopolitan town with a mix of old-world charm and modern tourism.
- It remains famous for its handcrafted marquetry (wood inlay art), delicious cuisine, and breathtaking views of the Bay of Naples.

### 3.4.2 Best Things to Do in Sorrento

### 🏛 Explore Piazza Tasso – The Lively Heart of Sorrento

Piazza Tasso is the main square of Sorrento, buzzing with activity, cafés, restaurants, and historic buildings.

- Named after Torquato Tasso, a famous 16th-century poet born in Sorrento.
- A great place to people-watch while sipping espresso or Limoncello.
- Close to historic sites like the Church of Santa Maria del Carmine, which features a beautiful Baroque interior.

### 🏞 Admire the Views from Villa Comunale Park

One of the best panoramic viewpoints in Sorrento, Villa Comunale Park offers breathtaking views of Mount Vesuvius, the Bay of Naples, and Capri.

- A perfect spot for sunset watching and capturing postcard-worthy photos.
- Nearby is the Church of San Francesco, known for its serene cloisters.
- An elevator or stairs lead down to Marina Piccola, where boats depart for Capri.

### 🏺 Visit the Museo Correale di Terranova

Housed in an 18th-century villa, this museum showcases Neapolitan art, ceramics, and furniture from the 16th to 19th centuries.

- Features a collection of ancient Roman artifacts and local crafts.

- The museum's terrace garden offers stunning sea views.
- A must-visit for art lovers and history enthusiasts.

### 🍋 Taste Limoncello – Sorrento's Iconic Lemon Liqueur

Sorrento is world-famous for its lemons, and Limoncello, a sweet and tangy liqueur, is one of the best souvenirs you can take home.

- Visit I Giardini di Cataldo, a family-run lemon grove offering tours and tastings.
- Try Limoncello-based desserts, gelato, and cocktails at local cafés.
- Many shops offer free samples, so be sure to stop by for a taste.

### ⛵ Take a Boat Trip to Capri

Sorrento is one of the best departure points for Capri, with frequent ferry connections to the island's Blue Grotto and Marina Grande.

- A day trip to Capri allows you to explore charming towns, sea caves, and stunning coastal views.
- Private boat tours provide a luxurious and intimate experience of the island.

### 🛶 Relax at Marina Grande & Marina Piccola

Sorrento has two beautiful harbors that offer a mix of beach relaxation and waterfront dining.

- Marina Grande – A quaint fishing village with beachfront restaurants serving fresh seafood.
- Marina Piccola – A lively port area where ferries depart for Naples and Capri.

## 3.4.3 Best Places to Stay in Sorrento

### 🏨 Luxury Hotels

- Grand Hotel Excelsior Vittoria – A 5-star historic hotel with panoramic views and Michelin-star dining.
- Bellevue Syrene – A cliffside retreat with elegant decor and stunning sea views.

### 🛏 Mid-Range & Boutique Stays

- Maison La Minervetta – A stylish boutique hotel with a modern Mediterranean vibe.
- Hotel Antiche Mura – A charming hotel near Piazza Tasso with a peaceful garden and lemon grove.

### 🏠 Budget-Friendly Options

- Ulisse Deluxe Hostel – A comfortable and budget-friendly stay near the town center.
- Casa Sorrentina – A family-run B&B offering a cozy and authentic Sorrentine experience.

## 3.4.4 Tips for Visiting Sorrento

✔ Use Sorrento as a Base for Exploring – It's well-connected to Naples, Capri, Pompeii, and the Amalfi Coast.

✔ Visit in Spring or Fall – Summer can be extremely crowded and hot. April-June & September-October offer the best weather.

✔ Try Local Cuisine – Don't miss Gnocchi alla Sorrentina (baked gnocchi with tomato and mozzarella) and Sfogliatella pastry.

✔ Book Hotels in Advance – Sorrento is a popular destination, and the best accommodations sell out quickly.

✔ Be Prepared for Hills & Steps – The town has steep streets, so bring comfortable walking shoes.

Sorrento is much more than a gateway to the Amalfi Coast—it is a destination rich in history, culture, and natural beauty. With its stunning coastal views, charming old town, and world-famous lemons, Sorrento provides a perfect mix of relaxation, adventure, and Italian charm. Whether you're here for the scenic landscapes, the lively piazzas, or the incredible food, Sorrento promises an unforgettable experience on the Amalfi Coast.

# Chapter 4. Top Attractions & Landmarks

## 4.1 Path of the Gods Hike (Sentiero degli Dei)

A Journey Through Myth and Majestic Vistas
  The Path of the Gods, known locally as Sentiero degli Dei, is far more than a mere hiking trail—it's an immersive expedition that weaves together ancient legends, historical lore, and some of the most awe-inspiring coastal panoramas in the world. According to local myth, this trail was once trodden by the Greek gods themselves, on a quest to rescue the hero Ulysses from the enchanting sirens of the coast. Today, this storied route offers hikers a chance to traverse a landscape steeped in mythology while enjoying uninterrupted views of the Tyrrhenian Sea, the majestic island of Capri, and the rugged Amalfi coastline.

Trail Experience and Highlights
  Embarking on this hike means ascending clifftop pathways that reveal a tapestry of terraced vineyards, vibrant wildflower patches, and ancient stone dwellings that whisper tales of bygone eras. The trail's ever-changing terrain—from gentle slopes near its start to steep, challenging sections further along—ensures that every step offers a new visual delight.

- Breathtaking Panoramas: As you make your way along the trail, you're treated to stunning cliffside views that frame the shimmering

Mediterranean below. The vistas provide a continuous panorama of coastal beauty, making it one of the most photogenic hikes in Europe.
- Cultural Echoes: Along the way, remnants of traditional rural life emerge in the form of centuries-old shepherd huts, vineyards, and lemon groves. These features not only add to the scenic charm but also offer a glimpse into the enduring lifestyle of the Amalfi Coast's inhabitants.
- Notable Landmarks:
    - *Grotta del Biscotto:* This intriguing cave, named for its brittle, biscuit-like rock formations, houses ancient rock dwellings that hint at the lives of hermit monks and shepherds who once sought refuge here.
    - *Montepertuso Rock Formation:* A natural arch that local lore suggests was once pierced by the Virgin Mary, adding a layer of spiritual mystique to your journey.
    - *Nocelle Village:* The trail culminates in this quaint hilltop hamlet, which sits high above the bustling town of Positano. From here, adventurous hikers can opt to descend over 1,500 stone steps to reach the beach or catch a local bus back to the town center.

Location and Access

- Starting Point: The hike begins in the charming village of Bomerano, part of the Agerola area. This starting point is ideal for those seeking a peaceful, rural setting before the trail gradually ascends into more rugged terrain.
- Ending Point: The journey concludes in Nocelle, perched above the iconic town of Positano, where you can either make the long descent on foot or use local transport for a more relaxed return.
- How to Get There:
    - *From Naples:* Take a train to Sorrento, then a bus to Agerola (Bomerano).
    - *From Amalfi:* Board a SITA bus directly to Agerola.
    - *From Positano:* If ending your hike in Nocelle, you can either descend by foot or catch a local bus.

Practical Details

- Cost: The trail itself is free to access; however, guided tours are available at varying prices, typically ranging from €30 to €80 per person.
- Best Time to Hike: Although the Path of the Gods is open year-round, the optimal times for hiking are during the spring (April–June) and fall (September–October). These periods offer milder weather and fewer crowds, enhancing your overall experience.
- Trail Difficulty: This moderate hike spans approximately 8 km (around 5 miles) and typically takes 2.5 to 3.5 hours to complete, with an elevation gain of about 650 meters (roughly 2,100 feet) during the descent into Positano. It features some rocky sections, so proper footwear and hiking gear are essential.

Essential Hiking Tips

- Footwear: Invest in sturdy, well-fitting hiking boots as the trail includes rocky and sometimes slippery sections.
- Hydration & Snacks: Carry ample water and high-energy snacks since there are few places to purchase supplies along the way.
- Start Early: Begin your hike at sunrise to avoid the midday heat, particularly during the summer months.
- Weather Preparedness: Check local weather forecasts before setting out, as conditions can change rapidly—rain or fog can make parts of the trail treacherous.
- Be Alert for Local Livestock: Keep an eye out for mules and other animals still used by local farmers for transport.

Conclusion

The Path of the Gods is an enchanting trail that offers a blend of myth, history, and natural splendor. Every step on this legendary path provides a sensory feast—from the aroma of wildflowers and the rustling of ancient olive groves to the breathtaking vistas of the Mediterranean. Whether you're drawn by its storied past, the challenge of its rugged terrain, or simply the desire to experience one of the Amalfi Coast's most iconic hikes, the Path of the Gods promises an unforgettable adventure. For a comprehensive guide and additional resources, visit the official tourism websites and check weather updates to ensure a safe and rewarding journey through what many consider a slice of paradise on earth.

## 4.2 Villa Rufolo & Villa Cimbrone – Timeless Treasures of Ravello

Where History and Beauty Embrace

Perched majestically above the sparkling waters of the Amalfi Coast in the enchanting town of Ravello, Villa Rufolo and Villa Cimbrone stand as enduring symbols of Italian elegance and rich cultural heritage. These two historic villas, each with its own captivating story, offer visitors a unique journey into a world where art, history, and breathtaking natural beauty converge.

Villa Rufolo – A Symphony of Art and Music

Dating back to the 13th century, Villa Rufolo was originally built by the influential Rufolo family, one of Amalfi's most powerful merchant dynasties. This villa quickly became a beacon for artists, aristocrats, and scholars. Its timeless gardens, famed for inspiring the German composer Richard Wagner—who incorporated the villa's lush, enchanting scenery into his opera "Parsifal"—remain a major cultural magnet. Today, Villa Rufolo is not only a testament to medieval ingenuity but also a vibrant venue that hosts the renowned Ravello Festival, where classical music and art come together in an open-air celebration against a backdrop of sweeping sea views.

Key highlights of Villa Rufolo include:
- Stunning Gardens: Meticulously landscaped terraces bursting with vibrant flowers and verdant foliage that create an idyllic setting.
- Moorish Courtyard: Architectural details that reveal a blend of Arab, Norman, and Sicilian influences, echoing centuries of cultural exchange.
- Medieval Tower: A 30-meter-high tower that offers panoramic vistas of the Amalfi Coast and serves as a symbol of the villa's storied past.
- Festival Stage: The open-air venue that hosts performances during the Ravello Festival, where music and nature merge harmoniously.

Villa Cimbrone – A Dreamlike Retreat

Villa Cimbrone's origins stretch back to the 11th century, though much of its current grandeur was shaped in the 20th century by Lord William Beckett, who transformed the villa into a romantic hideaway. Its most celebrated feature, the Terrace of Infinity (Terrazza dell'Infinito), is renowned worldwide for its dramatic, uninterrupted views of the Mediterranean. Strolling along this terrace, lined with elegant marble busts, you are treated to a vista so expansive it seems as if the sea and sky are one. Villa Cimbrone also boasts a serene cloister, a charming tea room surrounded by a rose garden, and a mysterious crypt that hints at the villa's layered past.

Key highlights of Villa Cimbrone include:
- Terrace of Infinity: A breathtaking lookout that offers one of Italy's most famous panoramic views, where the vast expanse of the sea meets the rugged coastline.
- Medieval Cloister: A tranquil courtyard with Gothic architectural elements, perfect for quiet reflection.
- Elegant Tea Room & Rose Garden: A picturesque setting ideal for enjoying a leisurely break, complete with delicate floral arrangements and softly flowing water features.
- Historic Crypt: A mysterious underground chamber that adds a touch of enigma to the villa's rich history.

Location and Access

Both villas are located in the heart of Ravello, an ancient town renowned for its artistic and historical significance.
- Villa Rufolo: Situated in Piazza Duomo, 84010 Ravello SA, Italy (GPS: 40.6502° N, 14.6105° E).
- Villa Cimbrone: Located on Via Santa Chiara, 26, 84010 Ravello SA, Italy (GPS: 40.6536° N, 14.6124° E).

Getting to Ravello is straightforward: you can reach it by taking a SITA bus from Amalfi or Positano, or by driving along the picturesque coastal roads, with paid parking available in Piazza Duomo.

Admission and Visiting Hours
- Villa Rufolo: Typically charges an entry fee of €8 per person (discounts for students and seniors), and is open from 9:00 AM to 7:00 PM from March to October, with reduced hours in the winter.
- Villa Cimbrone: Charges about €10 per person (discounts for students and seniors), and is open from 9:00 AM to 8:00 PM during the warmer months, closing earlier in winter.

A Unique Cultural Experience

Visiting these historic villas is like stepping into a living museum, where every stone and every garden tells a story of the past. Both properties not only offer spectacular views and lush gardens but also serve as cultural centers hosting concerts, art exhibitions, and educational tours. They capture the essence of the Amalfi Coast, where the legacy of the past enriches the present, and every visit is an opportunity to experience the romance and grandeur of Italian heritage.

Conclusion

Whether you are captivated by the melodic history of Villa Rufolo or the dreamlike vistas from Villa Cimbrone's Terrace of Infinity, both villas represent the soul of Ravello. They offer a perfect blend of historical significance, artistic inspiration, and natural beauty that makes a visit to the Amalfi Coast truly unforgettable. From intimate guided tours and live performances to serene moments of reflection amid lush gardens, these timeless jewels invite you to explore the enchanting legacy of the Amalfi Coast in all its splendor.

For further details and planning your visit, check their official websites:
- Villa Rufolo: [villarufolo.it](villarufolo.it)
- Villa Cimbrone: [villacimbrone.com](villacimbrone.com)

## 4.3 Cathedral of Amalfi & Paper Museum – A Journey Through Faith and Craftsmanship

### A Tale of Legacy and Innovation

Tucked within the heart of **Amalfi**, where medieval alleys whisper stories of a once-mighty maritime republic, two historical gems stand as testaments to its rich past—the **Cathedral of Amalfi** and the **Amalfi Paper Museum (Museo della Carta)**.

The **Cathedral of St. Andrew (Duomo di Amalfi)** is a striking fusion of **Arab-Norman, Byzantine, Gothic, and Baroque architecture**, reflecting centuries of cultural influence. Originally built in the **9th century**, it houses the relics of **St. Andrew, the patron saint of Amalfi**, and remains an important pilgrimage site. Its imposing **grand staircase**, stunning **cloister**, and intricate **gold-leaf mosaics** make it one of the most breathtaking religious landmarks in southern Italy.

Just a short walk from the cathedral lies the **Amalfi Paper Museum**, a tribute to the town's **ancient papermaking industry**. Dating back to the **12th century**, Amalfi was a pioneer in **handmade paper production**, rivaling the finest parchment of the time. Inside the museum, visitors can witness **centuries-old mills, traditional machinery, and live demonstrations**, gaining a glimpse into the delicate art that shaped Amalfi's legacy in literature and commerce.

Together, these sites offer a **deep dive into Amalfi's spiritual, artistic, and industrial past**, making them essential stops for travelers seeking history beyond the coastline's beauty.

📍 **Location**

### Cathedral of Amalfi (Duomo di Sant'Andrea)

- **Address:** Piazza Duomo, 84011 Amalfi SA, Italy
- **GPS Coordinates:** 40.6344° N, 14.6020° E

### Amalfi Paper Museum (Museo della Carta)

- **Address:** Via delle Cartiere, 23, 84011 Amalfi SA, Italy
- **GPS Coordinates:** 40.6361° N, 14.6033° E

### How to Get There

- **From Positano:** Take a **ferry or SITA bus** (~40 minutes).
- **From Ravello:** A **20-minute bus ride** or a scenic **hike down via Valle delle Ferriere**.
- **By Car:** Parking is available in **Luna Rossa Parking Garage**, a **10-minute walk** from both sites.

### Price & Entry Fee

**Cathedral of Amalfi**

- **Entry Fee:** €3 per person (**includes access to the cloister, crypt, and museum**)
- **Children under 6:** Free

**Amalfi Paper Museum**

- **Entry Fee:** €4 per person
- **Guided Tour (with demonstration):** €5 per person

### Opening Hours

**Cathedral of Amalfi**

- **April – October:** 9:00 AM – 6:45 PM
- **November – March:** 10:00 AM – 5:00 PM
- **Sunday Mass:** 8:00 AM, 10:00 AM, 6:00 PM

**Amalfi Paper Museum**

- **Daily:** 10:00 AM – 6:30 PM

## ✹ Key Features
### ♜ Cathedral of Amalfi Highlights

✔ **The Grand Staircase:** A dramatic **62-step stairway** leading to the cathedral's entrance.
✔ **The Cloister of Paradise:** An **Arabesque courtyard** lined with **slender marble columns and Moorish arches**.
✔ **The Crypt of St. Andrew:** A sacred chamber housing the **relics of St. Andrew**, brought to Amalfi from Constantinople in **1208**.
✔ **The Bronze Doors:** Cast in **Constantinople in 1066**, they are among the oldest **Byzantine doors** in Italy.
✔ **The Mosaic Façade:** A shimmering **gold-leaf Byzantine mosaic**, depicting **Christ enthroned**.

### 📜 Amalfi Paper Museum Highlights

✔ **12th-Century Water Mills:** Original **hydraulic mills** used for paper production.
✔ **Ancient Presses & Tools: Wooden mallets, vats, and sieves** once used by medieval artisans.
✔ **Live Demonstrations:** Visitors can **watch and participate** in the **traditional papermaking process**.
✔ **Historical Manuscripts:** Display of **handmade Amalfi paper** used in **royal and papal documents**.
✔ **Shop & Souvenirs:** Purchase **authentic Amalfi paper** and handcrafted stationery.

## 🛠 Visitor Services

✔ **Gift Shops & Bookstores** – Available at both sites.
✔ **Audio Guides & Guided Tours** – Offered in multiple languages.
✔ **Restrooms & Visitor Facilities** – Available at both locations.
✔ **Accessibility:** The cathedral has **ramps and an elevator**, but the museum's **upper levels are not wheelchair-accessible**.

## Detailed Description
### Cathedral of Amalfi – A Spiritual Masterpiece

The **Duomo di Amalfi** is an architectural **marvel that reflects centuries of transformation**. The **grand staircase** leading up to the cathedral, often bustling with visitors, is a stunning **introduction to its magnificence**. The **bronze doors**, commissioned in **1066 by a wealthy merchant in Constantinople**, are some of the oldest in Italy.

Inside, the **interior dazzles with gilded ceilings, intricate frescoes, and marble inlays**. One of the highlights is the **Cloister of Paradise**, built in the **13th century**, which once served as a burial site for Amalfi's aristocrats. Its elegant Moorish-style **arches and columns** are a **testament to the region's Arab influence**.

Deep within the cathedral lies the **Crypt of St. Andrew**, where the relics of **Jesus' first apostle** are enshrined. The crypt, **adorned with golden frescoes and marble sculptures**, is a place of **spiritual significance**, drawing both pilgrims and history enthusiasts alike.

### Amalfi Paper Museum – The Art of Handmade Paper

The **Amalfi Paper Museum** transports visitors back to an era when **handmade paper was a precious commodity**, used for **legal documents, religious texts, and royal decrees**. Housed in a **12th-century paper mill**, the museum preserves **centuries-old techniques of papermaking**.

The guided tour begins with an **explanation of the ancient process**—raw materials like **cotton and linen rags** were pulped using **massive wooden mallets** powered by **water mills**. Visitors can see the **original machines**

**in motion**, demonstrating how Amalfi's artisans **crafted sheets of paper by hand**.

A fascinating highlight is the **live papermaking demonstration**, where guests can participate in **creating their own Amalfi paper**, following the same **immersion and drying techniques used for centuries**. The museum also showcases **handwritten royal letters, parchment scrolls, and antique printing presses**, offering a **rare glimpse into medieval book production**.

### 🔗 Official Websites & Additional Resources

- **Cathedral of Amalfi:** www.amalficathedral.com
- **Amalfi Paper Museum:** www.museodellacarta.it

Visiting the **Cathedral of Amalfi and the Paper Museum** is an **unforgettable journey through history, faith, and craftsmanship**. The **duomo's breathtaking mosaics, relics, and cloisters** transport you to **a time of grandeur and devotion**, while the **museum's preserved mills and interactive demonstrations** immerse you in **a centuries-old tradition of artistry**.

For those seeking to experience **the deeper soul of Amalfi beyond its stunning coastline**, these two sites offer a **profound and enriching cultural experience**.

## 4.4 Emerald Grotto & Fiordo di Furore – Nature's Hidden Wonders on the Amalfi Coast

### A Tale of Two Natural Wonders

Nestled between towering cliffs along the rugged coastline of the Amalfi Coast, the **Emerald Grotto (Grotta dello Smeraldo)** and the **Fiordo di Furore** are two of the region's most stunning natural wonders. Both sites offer a unique glimpse into the raw beauty of the Mediterranean, where the forces of nature have shaped dramatic landscapes over centuries.

The **Emerald Grotto** is a subterranean sea cave famous for its luminous green waters, which glow with an ethereal light when the sun's rays penetrate the cave through an underwater opening. Discovered in the 1930s by a local fisherman, this grotto has since become one of the most sought-after natural attractions on the coast, drawing visitors eager to witness the mesmerizing effect of light filtering through the crystal-clear waters.

Just a short distance away is the **Fiordo di Furore**, a breathtaking fjord that cuts deep into the cliffs, forming a narrow inlet between steep, towering rock walls. This secluded spot is home to one of Italy's most famous beaches and a hidden village perched on the cliffs. The dramatic scenery and unique geography make the Fiordo di Furore an unforgettable part of any Amalfi Coast itinerary.

These two wonders—one submerged beneath the waves and the other nestled in the cliffs—are the epitome of nature's artistry on the Amalfi Coast, offering visitors an unparalleled experience of the region's natural beauty.

## Location

### Emerald Grotto (Grotta dello Smeraldo)

- **Address:** Via Grotte di Seiano, 84010 Conca dei Marini SA, Italy
- **GPS Coordinates:** 40.6130° N, 14.5740° E

### Fiordo di Furore

- **Address:** Via Furore, 84010 Furore SA, Italy
- **GPS Coordinates:** 40.6241° N, 14.5983° E

## How to Get There

- **From Positano:** Both attractions are easily accessible by **SITA bus** (around 20 minutes). Alternatively, **private car rentals** or **taxi services** can take you to both locations.
- **From Ravello:** The **Emerald Grotto** is around a **30-minute drive** via **SS163**, while the **Fiordo di Furore** is a **25-minute drive**.
- **By Boat:** The **Emerald Grotto** can also be reached by boat, with tours departing from **Amalfi** and **Positano**.

## Price & Entry Fee

### Emerald Grotto (Grotta dello Smeraldo)

- **Entry Fee:** €5 per person for the boat tour into the grotto

- **Children (under 6):** Free

**Fiordo di Furore**

- **Entry Fee:** Free to visit the fiord and view from the cliffs
- **Beach Access:** There is a small **entrance fee for access to the beach**, approximately **€5**

● **Opening Hours**

**Emerald Grotto (Grotta dello Smeraldo)**

- **March – October:** 9:00 AM – 7:00 PM
- **November – February:** 9:00 AM – 4:00 PM (weather permitting)

**Fiordo di Furore**

- **Open year-round:** 24 hours
- **Beach access** is typically available from **June to September**, depending on weather conditions.

✸ **Key Features**
**Emerald Grotto Highlights**

✔ **Green Glow:** The grotto's waters glow in a vibrant **emerald hue**, caused by sunlight filtering through an underwater opening.
✔ **Boat Tours:** Visitors can board **small boats** to explore the cave and marvel at the unusual green lighting.
✔ **Crystal-Clear Waters:** The **grotto's depths** are home to diverse marine life, making it a peaceful and enchanting experience.
✔ **Stalactites and Stalagmites:** The cave's interior is decorated with natural **formations** of stalactites and stalagmites.
✔ **Underwater Entrance:** The cave's entrance is only accessible by **boat**, adding a sense of adventure to the visit.

**Fiordo di Furore Highlights**

✔ **Secluded Fjord:** A **narrow inlet** surrounded by towering cliffs, offering dramatic views of the coastline.

✔ **Scenic Beach:** Known for its **secluded beach** nestled at the foot of the cliffs, the Fiordo di Furore is perfect for a quiet dip in the Mediterranean.
✔ **Hidden Village:** The tiny **Furore village** is perched on the cliffside, its colorful houses offering stunning views of the fjord.
✔ **Cliffside Views:** The fjord offers **panoramic views** from the surrounding cliffs, with visitors able to hike down or view from above.
✔ **Famous for Cliff Diving:** The fjord is a renowned spot for **cliff diving**, hosting annual competitions, which makes it an attraction for adventure seekers.

## 🛠 Visitor Services

✔ **Emerald Grotto:**

- **Gift shop and souvenir stand** at the grotto entrance.
- **Boats with local guides** available for tours.
- **Restrooms and seating** available near the boat dock.

✔ **Fiordo di Furore:**

- **Beach café and restaurant** offering local Amalfi Coast cuisine.
- **Public restrooms** located near the beach.
- **Parking:** Limited parking available along the road leading to the fiord.
- **Cliffside Viewing Areas: Benches and observation points** on the surrounding cliffs for spectacular panoramic views.

## 📕 Detailed Description
### Emerald Grotto – A Glowing Submarine Wonderland

The **Emerald Grotto** is one of the most magical spots along the Amalfi Coast. The cave was first discovered in the **1930s by a local fisherman**, who noticed a faint glow emanating from the cave. It wasn't long before it became a **popular tourist attraction**, with its stunning green waters captivating all who visited.

The grotto's ethereal glow is caused by sunlight filtering through an **underwater opening**, reflecting off the sea bed and creating the **emerald hue**. This natural phenomenon, combined with the grotto's **tranquil waters and ancient rock formations**, gives visitors the sensation of being submerged in a world of calm and mystery. The boat tours into the cave are short but memorable, offering the chance to take in the **stalactites and stalagmites** that line the cave's walls. The grotto is accessible only by boat, and while there are no swimming opportunities within the cave itself, the experience of navigating the small boats through the dimly lit waters is unforgettable.

**Fiordo di Furore – The Hidden Fjord of the Amalfi Coast**

The **Fiordo di Furore** is a unique geological formation, where a fjord-like inlet carves its way through **steep cliffs**, creating a dramatic contrast of land and sea. The fiord is both a **breathtaking viewpoint** and an active location, where visitors can enjoy the views from above or venture down to the beach for a peaceful retreat.

The beach at Fiordo di Furore is accessible via **stairs and paths**, offering a sense of seclusion that makes it one of the **most peaceful beaches** on the Amalfi Coast. The surrounding cliffs are perfect for **cliff diving**, and the fiord is often the site of **international competitions** where daring athletes leap from the cliffs into the waters below.

The village of **Furore**, perched above the fiord, is a hidden gem on the Amalfi Coast. The village's **colorful houses** stand in stark contrast to the surrounding natural landscape, offering picturesque views over the water. **Local restaurants and cafés** serve delicious Amalfi Coast specialties, and visitors can wander the narrow lanes of the village to experience the unique atmosphere of this secluded place.

### 🔗 Official Websites & Additional Resources

- **Emerald Grotto:** [www.grottadellosmeraldo.it](www.grottadellosmeraldo.it)
- **Fiordo di Furore:** No official website, but more information can be found through local tourism sites and guides.

The **Emerald Grotto** and **Fiordo di Furore** are two of the Amalfi Coast's **most remarkable natural wonders**. The grotto enchants with its **glowing waters**, while the fiord offers visitors a chance to experience **rugged cliffs and serene beaches**. Whether you're exploring the mysterious green-lit cave or enjoying the dramatic coastal landscape at the fiord, these sites provide a deeper connection to the wild beauty of the Amalfi Coast.

## 4.5 Marina Grande & Hidden Beaches – The Amalfi Coast's Scenic Seaside Retreats

### A Seaside Haven of Sun and Serenity

The Amalfi Coast is not only known for its dramatic cliffs and colorful towns, but also for its **beautiful beaches**, and among the most famous is **Marina Grande** in **Positano**. This charming beach is a perfect example of the Amalfi Coast's harmonious blend of nature, culture, and luxury. Marina Grande is a **bustling yet serene beach**, offering visitors a lively atmosphere with sunbeds, vibrant cafés, and stunning views of the cliffside village rising above the coast.

But the Amalfi Coast also holds secrets, and nestled along the coastline, **hidden beaches** offer more seclusion and tranquility. These beaches, often tucked away in coves or accessible only by boat, provide an opportunity to escape the crowds and embrace the quiet beauty of the Mediterranean. Whether you're visiting the well-known Marina Grande or discovering one of the **hidden gems**, the Amalfi Coast's beaches are a place to unwind and soak in the region's unparalleled charm.

## Location

**Marina Grande**

- **Address:** Via Marina Grande, 84017 Positano SA, Italy
- **GPS Coordinates:** 40.6263° N, 14.4885° E

**Hidden Beaches (Various Locations)**

- **Spiaggia di Laurito (Positano)**

  - **Address:** Via Laurito, 84017 Positano SA, Italy
  - **GPS Coordinates:** 40.6120° N, 14.4935° E
- **Fornillo Beach (Positano)**

  - **Address:** Via Fornillo, 84017 Positano SA, Italy
  - **GPS Coordinates:** 40.6258° N, 14.4887° E
- **Arienzo Beach (Positano)**

  - **Address:** Via Arienzo, 84017 Positano SA, Italy
  - **GPS Coordinates:** 40.6273° N, 14.4856° E

- **Marina di Praia (Praiano)**

    - **Address:** Via Marina di Praia, 84010 Praiano SA, Italy
    - **GPS Coordinates:** 40.5994° N, 14.4796° E
- **Cala di Fornillo (Positano)**

    - **Address:** 84017 Positano SA, Italy
    - **GPS Coordinates:** 40.6255° N, 14.4891° E

## 💰 Price & Entry Fee

### Marina Grande

- **Public Access:** Free
- **Sunbed Rentals:** €20-€40 per day, depending on the season and location of the bed.
- **Beach Umbrella Rental:** €10-€20 per day

### Hidden Beaches

- **Spiaggia di Laurito:** Free to access, though boat rentals are available to reach the beach from Positano.
- **Fornillo Beach:** Free, though sunbeds and umbrellas can be rented for around **€20-€40**.
- **Arienzo Beach:** Free, but **boat access** from Positano is suggested, or visitors can take a long hike down to the beach.
- **Marina di Praia:** Free entry, with **restaurant access** offering sunbeds and umbrellas for rent.
- **Cala di Fornillo:** Free to visit, though **private boat tours** or **taxi boats** may be necessary for access.

## 🌑 Opening Hours

### Marina Grande

- **Open year-round:** 24/7
- **Best Visiting Hours:** 9:00 AM – 7:00 PM, especially during the summer months when restaurants and cafés are bustling.

**Hidden Beaches**

- **Spiaggia di Laurito & Fornillo Beach:** Accessible year-round, but the peak season for beachgoers is from **June to September**.
- **Arienzo Beach & Marina di Praia:** Best visited from **May to September** when the weather is ideal for sunbathing and swimming.
- **Cala di Fornillo:** Accessible year-round but can be difficult to reach in the winter due to weather conditions.

## 🌟 Key Features

**Marina Grande Highlights**

✔ **Vibrant Atmosphere:** The beach is famous for its lively cafés and **restaurants** that line the shore, offering **fresh seafood** and **local dishes**.
✔ **Panoramic Views:** Visitors can enjoy stunning views of **Positano's cliffside buildings** and the shimmering Mediterranean Sea.
✔ **Boating and Water Activities: Boat tours, paddleboarding, and kayaking** are popular activities at the beach, along with **private boat rentals** to explore the coast.
✔ **Lively Summer Events:** Marina Grande hosts **beach parties**, **live music**, and various **cultural events** during the summer months.
✔ **Public Beach:** Free access to the beach with plenty of space for sunbathing.

**Hidden Beaches Highlights**

✔ **Seclusion and Privacy:** These hidden beaches offer a more **quiet retreat**, away from the crowds, for those seeking solitude and relaxation.
✔ **Crystal-Clear Waters:** The beaches are known for their **pristine waters**, perfect for swimming and snorkeling in the Mediterranean.
✔ **Accessible by Boat:** Most hidden beaches can be accessed by **boat tours**, providing a unique perspective of the coastline and secret coves.
✔ **Natural Beauty:** These secluded spots are surrounded by **rugged cliffs** and **lush greenery**, making them a true natural paradise.
✔ **Exclusive Charm:** Many of these hidden beaches are only reachable by boat or long walks, making them more **exclusive** and peaceful.

## 🛠 Visitor Services

**Marina Grande**

✔ **Beachfront Restaurants & Bars:** Numerous spots to enjoy **Italian cuisine**, **cocktails**, and **coffee** with a view of the sea.
✔ **Boat Rentals:** Various **boat rental companies** offer **private boats** for exploring the coastline.
✔ **Sunbed & Umbrella Rentals:** Available at various locations, with prices varying based on the proximity to the water.
✔ **Public Restrooms:** Facilities available along the beach.
✔ **Beach Activities:** Kayaks, paddleboards, and small boats are available for rent.

**Hidden Beaches (Various Locations)**

✔ **Spiaggia di Laurito:** Small beach café offering **drinks and snacks** with a **shuttle boat service** from Positano.
✔ **Fornillo Beach: Beach bars** and **restaurants** offer local meals, alongside **sunbeds and umbrellas** for rent.
✔ **Arienzo Beach:** A **restaurant** serving traditional **Amalfi Coast cuisine**, with sunbeds and umbrellas for rent.
✔ **Marina di Praia: Bars and restaurants** overlooking the beach, where guests can enjoy fresh seafood.

✔ **Cala di Fornillo:** Best accessed by private boat or a **long walk** from the town, with **limited services** due to its secluded nature.

## Detailed Description
### Marina Grande – Positano's Heart and Soul

**Marina Grande** is the **main beach of Positano**, located just below the town's center. This **vibrant and lively beach** is the perfect place to begin your Amalfi Coast journey, as it offers stunning views of the colorful buildings cascading down the cliffs. The beach is typically lined with a variety of **restaurants**, where visitors can indulge in fresh seafood, pizza, or pasta while taking in the sea breeze. During summer, Marina Grande becomes the center of **Positano's social life**, with boat parties, live music, and cultural events filling the air. Despite the crowds, it's easy to find a quiet corner where you can **relax and unwind**, basking in the Mediterranean sun.

From Marina Grande, visitors can embark on boat tours, rent paddleboards, or simply swim in the crystal-clear water. It's also a great place to catch the **sight of the sun setting** over the sea, casting a golden hue over the cliffs and town.

### Hidden Beaches – Secluded Sanctuaries

For those seeking a more **tranquil and private beach experience**, the **hidden beaches** scattered along the Amalfi Coast provide the perfect escape. **Spiaggia di Laurito**, tucked between the cliffs, offers a peaceful retreat with **blue waters**, while **Fornillo Beach** provides a quieter alternative to Marina Grande. The **Arienzo Beach** and **Marina di Praia** are **accessible by boat**, offering secluded coves and pristine sands perfect for sunbathing and swimming. For the ultimate escape, **Cala di Fornillo** is a hidden gem that is **only accessible by boat**, giving visitors the chance to experience nature's untouched beauty.

## Official Websites & Additional Resources

- **Marina Grande (Positano):** No official website, but information can be found through **local tourism boards** and **Positano's official website**.

- **Spiaggia di Laurito & Fornillo Beach:** Local beaches with access information available at **Positano Tourism** or through **boat tour companies**.
- **Arienzo Beach & Marina di Praia:** More details can be found via **local tourism offices** or through private boat services for beach access.

The Amalfi Coast is home to some of the most spectacular beaches, whether it's the lively and picturesque **Marina Grande** or the secluded, tranquil **hidden beaches** that dot the coastline. Whether you prefer a **bustling beach atmosphere** with plenty of activities or a **quiet escape** surrounded by nature, you'll find the perfect spot to enjoy the **sun, sea, and serenity** that makes the Amalfi Coast a must-visit destination.

## 4.6 Ferriere Valley Nature Reserve – A Serene Escape into Nature

**A Journey Through Verdant Valleys and Historic Watermills**

The **Ferriere Valley Nature Reserve** offers a peaceful retreat for those looking to escape the crowds of the Amalfi Coast's more popular spots.

Hidden in the lush hills of **Ravello**, this reserve is a **natural haven** where visitors can immerse themselves in the region's pristine landscape. The reserve's name, "Ferriere," refers to the ancient **iron mills** that once dotted the valley, powered by the **fresh mountain streams** that still flow through today.

A place where **history and nature collide**, Ferriere Valley features a series of trails that lead through **forests**, along **rivers**, and past **historic mills**. The combination of **waterfalls**, **towering trees**, and remnants of ancient industry makes the Ferriere Valley an unforgettable destination. For those interested in a day surrounded by nature, this **protected area** offers a chance to experience the **wild beauty** of the Amalfi Coast, just a short distance from the more famous coastal towns.

## 📍 Location

- **Address:** Ferriere Valley Nature Reserve, 84010 Ravello SA, Italy
- **GPS Coordinates:** 40.6544° N, 14.5935° E

The reserve is located about **4 km** from Ravello's town center, nestled between **Ravello** and **Scala**, two historical towns that lie inland from the coast.

## 💰 Price & Entry Fee

- **Entrance Fee:** Free
- **Guided Tours (Optional):** Prices range from **€15 to €25** per person, depending on the tour provider and length of the hike.
- **Parking:** Available near the reserve entrance for a small fee, usually around **€2 to €5** per hour.

## ⚫ Opening Hours

- **Open Year-Round:**
    - **Best Visiting Hours:** 9:00 AM – 6:00 PM, although the reserve is open at all hours for hikers and nature lovers.
    - The best time to visit is from **April to October** when the weather is favorable for hiking and outdoor activities.

## ☀ Key Features

✔ **Hiking Trails:** The reserve features a range of hiking paths, from **easy** to **moderate** difficulty, with varying distances, making it suitable for all types of visitors.
✔ **Waterfalls & Streams:** Visitors can enjoy the soothing sounds of **cascading waterfalls** and **crystal-clear streams**. The reserve is home to several **natural springs** and historical mills powered by the flowing water.
✔ **Flora and Fauna:** Ferriere Valley is home to rich **biodiversity**, including **wildflowers**, **ferns**, and **ancient trees** like **chestnuts** and **holly**. Birdwatchers will also enjoy the abundance of **native bird species**, particularly in spring and summer.
✔ **Historical Mills:** The reserve features ancient **watermills** used for iron production and other industrial purposes in centuries past. The mills are an interesting glimpse into the area's **industrial history**.
✔ **Spectacular Views:** From the valley, hikers are treated to spectacular views of the **Amalfi Coast**, **Ravello**, and surrounding cliffs.

## 🛠 Visitor Services

✔ **Guided Tours:** Several tour companies offer **guided hikes** of the Ferriere Valley, which provide insight into the **local ecology**, **wildlife**, and the **history of the mills**.
✔ **Interpretive Signs:** Along the trails, visitors will find **informational signs** about the flora, fauna, and the history of the reserve.
✔ **Maps and Brochures:** Available at the entrance of the reserve or at the Ravello Tourist Information Office.
✔ **Rest Areas:** There are **benches** and **shaded spots** along the trails where visitors can rest and enjoy the views.
✔ **Public Restrooms:** Available near the reserve's entrance.
✔ **Parking:** There is a small parking lot at the entrance to the reserve, as well as parking options in Ravello.

## 📄 Detailed Description
### A Journey Through Nature

The **Ferriere Valley Nature Reserve** is one of the **Amalfi Coast's hidden gems**, offering a **calming contrast** to the busy coastal towns. As you enter the reserve, you're greeted by a refreshing **coolness** that comes from the surrounding trees and the **mountain streams**. The valley's landscape is deeply intertd with **history**, dating back to the **Roman and medieval periods**, when iron was produced using the energy from its powerful waterways.

The reserve is perfect for those who enjoy **nature walks**, **hiking**, and **bird watching**. There are several hiking routes to choose from, ranging from shorter trails that take you along the streams to longer, more challenging routes that ascend to the surrounding hills, providing **panoramic views** of the coast and **Mediterranean Sea**.

One of the key features of the Ferriere Valley is the **ancient watermills**. These structures were once used to **process iron** and **grind grain**, and some of them are still in remarkably good condition. They offer a fascinating look at the past industrial life of the region and provide a **historic backdrop** as you walk through the reserve.

The reserve is also home to an abundance of **flora and fauna**. You'll encounter numerous species of **wildflowers**, especially in spring, as well as large trees such as **chestnuts**, **oaks**, and **holly**. Keep an eye out for local wildlife, including **wild boar**, **deer**, and various types of **birds**, particularly in the spring and fall. The combination of nature and history makes Ferriere Valley a truly unique and enriching experience.

## 🔗 Official Websites & Additional Resources

- **Ferriere Valley Nature Reserve Information:** Ravello Tourism
- **Guided Tours & Hikes:** Available through local tour companies in Ravello or through the **Ravello Tourist Information Center**.

If you're a nature lover or history enthusiast, the **Ferriere Valley Nature Reserve** offers a serene and enriching experience. With its lush forests, historical mills, cascading waterfalls, and rich biodiversity, it's the perfect place to enjoy a **peaceful escape** into the heart of the **Amalfi Coast's natural beauty**. Whether you're hiking the trails, exploring the historical mills, or simply soaking in the views, Ferriere Valley promises a memorable day surrounded by the wonders of nature and history.

## 4.7 Sentiero degli Dei & Scenic Viewpoints – A Hiker's Paradise with Breathtaking Views

**A Legendary Trail Amidst the Clouds**

The **Sentiero degli Dei** (Path of the Gods) is one of the **most iconic hikes** along the Amalfi Coast, known for its spectacular panoramic views, dramatic cliffs, and tranquil surroundings. The trail's name is derived from the ancient belief that it was once walked by the gods who descended from the heavens to visit the coastal villages. Today, hikers are treated to views so divine that it's easy to understand why the path earned its celestial name.

The **Sentiero degli Dei** stretches from the **mountain village of Bomerano** near Agerola to **Nocelle**, just above Positano. It's a **moderately challenging** route, offering visitors the chance to immerse themselves in the stunning natural beauty of the region while getting a unique perspective of the coastline. With **wildflowers**, **rocky outcrops**, and **sweeping vistas**, this trail is a must for anyone who enjoys both adventure and breathtaking scenery.

### 📍 Location

- **Trailhead Locations:**
    - **Bomerano (Agerola):** This is the main starting point of the trail, accessible by bus or car.
    - **Nocelle (Positano):** The trail ends in Nocelle, a small village above Positano, offering views of the town below.
- **GPS Coordinates:** 40.6299° N, 14.4925° E (Bomerano)
- **Distance between Start and End:** 7.8 km (4.8 miles), approximately **3 to 5 hours** to complete depending on pace.

### 💰 Price & Entry Fee

- **Entrance Fee:** Free
- **Guided Tours (Optional):** Some local companies offer guided hiking tours, with prices ranging from **€30 to €50** per person, depending on the length of the hike and the services included.

- **Parking:** Paid parking is available at the trailheads in both **Bomerano** and **Nocelle**, usually around **€2 to €5** per hour.

## ● Opening Hours

- **Best Hiking Hours:** 8:00 AM – 5:00 PM, depending on the season. It's important to start early to avoid the midday heat, especially in the summer.
- **Best Time to Visit:** The trail is open year-round, but the best seasons are **spring** (March to May) and **fall** (September to November) when the weather is mild, and the landscape is lush. In summer, it can get quite hot, so it's advisable to hike early in the day.

## ✸ Key Features

✔ **Breathtaking Views:** The path is known for its **panoramic views** of the **Mediterranean Sea**, **Positano**, and the rugged Amalfi Coast cliffs. The high-altitude route offers visitors stunning vistas at every turn.

✔ **Historical Significance:** The trail has deep **historical roots**, often believed to be used by ancient gods, and its winding route connects **mountain villages** with the coast.

✔ **Flora and Fauna:** The trail offers the chance to see a range of **wildflowers**, **plants**, and local wildlife. In the spring, the area comes alive with **yellow broom** and **purple heather**, and hikers may spot **birds of prey** circling overhead.

✔ **Rocky Terrain & Dramatic Cliffs:** The trail is set against a backdrop of **rugged cliffs** and steep ravines, making for an exhilarating yet safe hiking experience.

✔ **Scenic Viewpoints:** Along the route, numerous **viewpoints** offer perfect spots for taking photos or simply resting while soaking in the mesmerizing landscape.

## 🛠 Visitor Services

✔ **Guided Tours:** Several tour companies offer **guided hikes** of the Sentiero degli Dei, often including transportation from Positano or Agerola. These tours provide insights into the **history, flora,** and **wildlife** along the trail.

✔ **Maps and Brochures:** Free maps are available at local **tourist information centers** in Positano, Agerola, and Ravello.
✔ **Rest Stops:** The path has occasional **rest areas** where you can take a break and enjoy a packed lunch with a view.
✔ **Public Restrooms:** Available at the trailheads in **Bomerano** and **Nocelle**.
✔ **Transportation: Public buses** run from **Agerola** (Bomerano) to **Positano** (Nocelle), making it easy for hikers to complete the hike one-way and return via bus.

## Detailed Description
### Hike of a Lifetime

The **Sentiero degli Dei** is an exhilarating hike that offers hikers a chance to **experience the Amalfi Coast from a unique angle**—from high above. Starting in the quiet mountain village of **Bomerano** (Agerola), the path leads through **breathtaking mountain landscapes**, lush vegetation, and rugged cliffs that drop dramatically into the turquoise sea below. The trail's path has been carved into the hillside, offering hikers constant views of the **Mediterranean** and **Positano**, the iconic cliffside town.

The **trail's terrain** is mostly uneven, with some rocky and narrow sections that require focus. But the effort is rewarded with **some of the best views** on the Amalfi Coast. Along the way, you'll encounter **wildflowers, oak trees**, and **ancient stone walls**, all while hearing the distant sound of the waves crashing below. The path itself is dotted with **scenic viewpoints**, where hikers can stop and take in **panoramic views** of the coast, **coves**, and **villages** that appear as if they were painted onto the cliffs.

The **Sentiero degli Dei** trail is a **moderate difficulty** hike, requiring a **reasonable level of fitness** to complete. Though the path is not difficult, the combination of the terrain and the altitude can challenge less experienced hikers. However, the trail is **well-marked**, and most people can manage it comfortably in **3 to 5 hours**, depending on their pace.

The end of the trail brings you to **Nocelle**, a charming village above Positano, offering a bird's-eye view of the town's iconic colorful houses. From here, you can enjoy the opportunity to either continue your journey down into **Positano** on foot or take a **bus** back to Agerola.

## 🔗 Official Websites & Additional Resources

- **Official Information:** Amalfi Coast Hiking
- **Guided Tours & Hikes:** Local companies such as **Walks of Italy** and **Amalfi Coast Hiking** offer guided tours along the Sentiero degli Dei.
- **Local Tourist Information:** Visit the **Positano Tourism Center** or **Agerola Visitor Center** for maps and further details.

The **Sentiero degli Dei** is a **bucket-list hike** for anyone visiting the Amalfi Coast. Whether you're an experienced hiker or just someone looking to enjoy nature from a new perspective, this trail offers a **once-in-a-lifetime experience**. With its **stunning views**, **rich history**, and **breathtaking landscapes**, it's easy to see why the **Path of the Gods** has earned its legendary status. Don't miss this iconic journey—it promises to be one of the highlights of your Amalfi Coast adventure.

# Chapter 5. Amalfi Coast Experiences & Activities

## 5.1 Boat Tours & Coastal Cruises – A Unique Way to Discover the Amalfi Coast by Sea

Sailing Through a World of Beauty and History
 Imagine gliding along the shimmering blue waters of the Tyrrhenian Sea while the dramatic cliffs and pastel villages of the Amalfi Coast unfold before your eyes. Boat tours and coastal cruises offer an exceptional way to experience this UNESCO World Heritage site from a completely different perspective. By taking to the water, visitors can explore hidden coves, pristine beaches, and secluded grottos that remain inaccessible by land, while also enjoying the gentle sea breeze and spectacular coastal panoramas.
Why Choose a Boat Tour?
 Opting for a boat tour or a coastal cruise means bypassing the challenges of navigating narrow, winding roads and dealing with limited parking, especially

during peak tourist seasons. Whether you're looking for a romantic evening sail, a private charter for a family gathering, or a guided group excursion that shares fascinating historical tales, there's a waterborne option to suit every taste. These cruises not only provide an immersive view of the Amalfi Coast's natural beauty but also offer insights into the rich maritime history and local legends that have shaped the region.

Departure Points and Accessibility

Boat tours on the Amalfi Coast typically depart from several key ports:
- Positano: Many tours begin at Positano's bustling marina, where boats set sail from the base of this iconic cliffside village.
- Amalfi: With its historic harbor, Amalfi serves as another popular launch point, offering easy connections to various coastal destinations.
- Ravello: Although not directly on the water, Ravello is linked to Amalfi by boat tours, giving visitors the chance to combine a hilltop cultural experience with a refreshing coastal journey.
- Minori & Maiori: These smaller, less crowded towns also provide access to boat excursions, offering a more tranquil and intimate experience.

Pricing and Options
- Group Tours: Shared public tours generally cost between €40 and €100 per person, with pricing varying based on tour duration, type, and included amenities.
- Private Charters: For those who desire an exclusive experience, private boat rentals offer a customizable itinerary. Prices for half-day charters typically range from €300 to €700, while full-day rentals can cost anywhere from €1,500 to €3,000.
- Luxury Cruises: For the ultimate indulgence, luxury cruises and private yacht charters, often featuring gourmet dining, live music, and personalized service, are available and can start at around €500, with some experiences exceeding €5,000 depending on the boat and services.

Optimal Times for a Cruise

Boat tours operate throughout the year, though the most favorable conditions occur during the peak season from May to October. The best experiences are often enjoyed in the early morning or late afternoon when the sunlight is softer and the sea is calmer. Sunset cruises, in particular, are a popular choice for their romantic ambiance and the chance to watch the coast bathed in the warm glow of the setting sun.

Key Features and Experiences

- Breathtaking Coastal Views: Enjoy uninterrupted, panoramic vistas of cliffside villages like Positano, Amalfi, and Ravello. The ever-changing scenery—vividly colored houses, lush vegetation, and dramatic rock formations—creates countless photo opportunities.
- Exploration of Hidden Gems: Many tours venture off the beaten path, leading you to secluded beaches, quiet coves, and mystical sea caves such as the Emerald Grotto, where the water glows with an otherworldly green hue.
- Cultural Insights: Guided boat tours often include commentary on the local maritime history, from ancient seafaring traditions to modern-day legends, providing context to the coastal beauty and enriching your experience.
- Leisure and Adventure: Whether you want to swim in the crystal-clear water, snorkel among marine life, or simply relax with a refreshing drink while enjoying the view, there is an option to suit every mood and interest.

Visitor Services

Most boat tour operators provide a range of services to ensure a comfortable and enjoyable journey:

- Onboard Refreshments: Complimentary beverages, such as local wines, limoncello, or sparkling water, are often served. Some tours may also offer light snacks or even a full meal on longer excursions.
- Convenient Transfers: Many companies offer pick-up and drop-off services from popular hotels and central locations, which adds to the convenience of your travel.
- Guided Experiences: Experienced guides lead many tours, sharing intriguing tales about the region's history, local legends, and natural features. This personal touch can make your cruise both informative and entertaining.
- Safety Measures: All operators adhere to strict safety standards, providing life jackets, emergency protocols, and regular maintenance of their vessels to ensure a secure journey.

Conclusion

Embarking on a boat tour or coastal cruise along the Amalfi Coast is not merely a mode of transportation—it's an integral part of the overall experience. From the thrill of discovering hidden beaches and mystical grottos to the leisurely pleasure of a sunset cruise, these maritime adventures reveal the true soul of the Amalfi Coast. By choosing from a range of tour options, from budget-friendly group tours to luxurious private charters, you can tailor your journey to match your preferences. Ultimately, setting sail along this spectacular coastline allows you to immerse yourself in the enchanting blend of natural beauty, rich history, and vibrant culture that defines the Amalfi Coast.

For more information on available tours and to book your adventure, be sure to visit official websites such as Positano Boat Tours or Amalfi Coast Cruises.

## 5.2 Tasting & Lemon Groves – Savoring the Flavors of the Amalfi Coast

A Journey Through Culinary and Agricultural Traditions

The Amalfi Coast is celebrated not only for its dramatic cliffside views and charming villages but also for its rich agricultural heritage. At the heart of this tradition lie the terraced vineyards and legendary lemon groves that define the region. These lush groves and carefully tended vineyards offer visitors a unique opportunity to immerse themselves in the local food culture, where every bite and sip tells a story of time-honored practices and the bounties of the Mediterranean sun.

Discovering the Local Produce

The fertile hillsides of the Amalfi Coast produce some of Italy's most distinctive citrus fruits and wines. The Sfusato Amalfitano lemon, renowned for its large size, aromatic zest, and perfectly balanced sweet-tart flavor, is a true coastal treasure. These lemons are the star ingredient in many local delicacies, from the tangy limoncello liqueur to lemon-infused desserts and savory dishes. Meanwhile, the vineyards, interlaced with ancient terraces and draped in vibrant bougainvillea, yield exceptional white wines such as Falanghina, Fiano, and Biancolella. These wines capture the essence of the Mediterranean climate, combining bright acidity with a delicate minerality that is truly unique to the region.

Tasting Tours: An Immersive Experience

Local tasting tours provide an immersive exploration into these culinary delights.

- Vineyard Tours: Many family-run vineyards offer guided tours where you can stroll among the vines, learn about the cultivation techniques passed down through generations, and sample a selection of freshly produced wines. These tours often conclude with a tasting session

paired with traditional regional cheeses, cured meats, and local bread, providing an authentic flavor of the coast.
- Lemon Grove Tours: A visit to a lemon grove is an essential part of the Amalfi experience. Guided tours of these groves reveal the meticulous process of growing and harvesting the famous Sfusato lemons. You'll learn about the ancient farming techniques that have been refined over centuries and discover the unique environmental factors that contribute to the lemons' distinctive taste. Many tours also include tastings of limoncello, lemon marmalade, and even lemon-based confections, offering a comprehensive insight into the region's citrus legacy.

Where to Go

The production of fine wines and succulent lemons is concentrated in key areas along the coast:
- Vineyards: Towns such as Ravello, Furore, and Tramonti are renowned for their vineyards that cling to the steep cliffs, offering spectacular views along with world-class wine.
- Lemon Groves: Iconic lemon groves can be found in Minori, Maiori, and Vietri sul Mare. These groves not only produce the celebrated Sfusato lemons but also provide a serene backdrop for tasting sessions and leisurely strolls among the trees.

Cost and Practical Information
- Tasting Tours: Prices for vineyard and wine tasting tours typically range between €30 and €70 per person, which often include guided visits, tasting sessions, and sometimes a light meal.
- Lemon Grove Visits: Tours focused on lemon groves are generally more affordable, usually between €10 and €25 per person. These tours may also offer demonstrations on lemon cultivation and processing.
- Combined Experiences: For those seeking the full sensory experience, some tour operators offer combined vineyard and lemon grove packages, with prices ranging from €50 to €100 per person depending on the duration and inclusions.

Visitor Services and Amenities

Many estates provide additional amenities to enhance your experience:
- Guided Tours: Expert guides offer detailed commentary on the history and production methods of local wines and lemons, enriching your visit with cultural insights.

- Tasting Rooms and Shops: Most vineyards and lemon groves feature tasting rooms where you can sample their best products. On-site shops allow you to purchase unique, locally made goods such as wines, limoncello, and handcrafted souvenirs.
- Outdoor Dining: Some estates also offer outdoor dining experiences where you can enjoy meals prepared with fresh, local ingredients, often paired with the estate's own wines or citrus products.

Summary

A visit to the Amalfi Coast is incomplete without indulging in its culinary treasures. Tasting tours and lemon grove visits offer a delightful fusion of history, agriculture, and gastronomy. Whether you're sipping a glass of local white wine amidst terraced vineyards or wandering through fragrant lemon groves and sampling homemade limoncello, these experiences provide a deeper appreciation of the region's agricultural traditions and rich flavors. In essence, the Amalfi Coast invites you on a sensory journey where every flavor reflects the beauty and heritage of this enchanting part of Italy.

## 5.3 Cooking Classes & Local Markets – A Deep Dive into Amalfi's Culinary Heritage

**Unleash the Flavors of the Amalfi Coast through Cooking and Markets**

The Amalfi Coast isn't just a feast for the eyes with its dramatic cliffs and sparkling waters; it's also a **paradise for food lovers**. The region's culinary scene is deeply rooted in its agricultural landscape, where fresh, **local produce** is harvested daily and transformed into mouthwatering dishes that have become legendary. Whether you're learning to craft **pasta** from scratch, making traditional **limoncello**, or exploring vibrant markets filled with fresh ingredients, cooking classes and local markets provide an immersive, hands-on experience of the Amalfi Coast's flavors.

📍 **Location**

- **Cooking Classes:**
    Cooking classes can be found in various towns along the Amalfi Coast, with a particularly strong presence in **Positano**, **Ravello**, **Minori**, and

**Amalfi**. Most classes are offered in **private homes**, **family-run restaurants**, or at **local cooking schools** with panoramic views of the coast.

- **Local Markets:**

    - **Amalfi Market:** Located in the heart of **Amalfi** town, this lively market offers a wide range of fresh produce, local cheeses, meats, and seafood. It's a great spot to find ingredients for your cooking class or simply enjoy the authentic atmosphere of a bustling local market.
    - **Maiori Market:** This market offers **seasonal vegetables**, **handmade pasta**, and **local olive oils** and s. It's known for its **cheese stalls** and the famous **Limoncello** stands where you can sample the local citrus-based liqueur.
    - **Minori & Ravello Markets:** Both towns have picturesque weekly markets, with Ravello hosting a famous local artisan market where you can buy regional delicacies and crafts.

## 💰 Price & Entry Fee

- **Cooking Classes:**
  Cooking classes vary in price depending on the location, duration, and meal included. Prices generally range from **€70 to €150** per person for a half-day class. Some full-day or specialty cooking experiences, such as **seafood classes** or **pasta-making workshops**, can cost anywhere from **€150 to €300** per person, with meals and pairings included.
    - **Group Cooking Classes:** Starting at **€70 to €100** per person, these classes generally include a shared meal at the end.
    - **Private Cooking Classes:** Starting at **€150 to €250** per person, these classes often provide a more personalized experience with a local chef or family member guiding you through the meal preparation.
- **Local Markets:**

- **Free Entry:** Entry to most local markets is free. The cost will depend on your purchases, from fresh fruits, vegetables, artisanal cheeses, olive oils, and handmade goods to ready-made meals or snacks at market stalls.
- **Market Tours:** If you opt for a guided market tour, which typically includes visits to local producers and tastings, prices range from **€50 to €100** per person, depending on the length of the tour.

### ● Opening Hours & Best Time to Go

- **Cooking Classes:**
  Cooking classes are typically available throughout the week, with most beginning around **10:00 AM** for morning sessions. Afternoon classes are also common, starting around **2:00 PM**.

  - **Best Time to Go:** The most authentic culinary experiences are often in **late spring to early autumn (May to October)**, when the region's markets are brimming with **seasonal produce**, and the weather is perfect for enjoying food outdoors.
  - **Cooking classes during the off-season (November to April)** can be a bit quieter but still offer intimate experiences with local chefs and families.

- **Local Markets:**

  - **Amalfi Market:** Open **daily** from **7:00 AM to 1:00 PM** (except Sundays).
  - **Maiori Market:** Held every **Tuesday morning**, from **8:00 AM to 1:00 PM**.
  - **Minori & Ravello Markets:** Open **weekly** (Ravello on **Thursdays**, Minori on **Fridays**) from **7:00 AM to 1:00 PM**.

### ✹ Key Features

✔ **Hands-on Cooking Classes:** From **making fresh pasta** to **preparing seafood dishes** like **Spaghetti alle Vongole**, cooking classes on the Amalfi Coast allow you to learn local techniques using fresh ingredients sourced from local markets.

✔ **Fresh, Local Ingredients:** Experience the unique flavors of the **Amalfi Coast's produce**, including **artichokes, tomatoes, garlic, fresh herbs**, and **seafood** such as anchovies and sardines.

✔ **Limoncello Making:** Many cooking schools offer classes that include learning how to make **limoncello**, the famous Amalfi Coast lemon liqueur, using the region's **Sfusato lemons**.

✔ **Market Tours:** Guided market tours not only teach you about local ingredients but also give you the opportunity to taste traditional street foods such as **pizza margherita, sfogliatella**, and **fresh mozzarella**.

✔ **Cultural Connection:** Cooking classes are often held in **family homes** or **historic locations**, allowing you to connect with local chefs, learn about their culinary traditions, and enjoy meals as part of the local community.

## 🛠 Visitor Services

✔ **Private and Group Classes:**

Cooking schools offer both **private and group sessions**, accommodating couples, families, or large groups. Private classes typically provide a more tailored experience, focusing on your specific interests (e.g., pasta-making or seafood preparation).

✔ **Local Market Tours:**

Guided market tours typically last **1.5 to 3 hours** and include a walk through the town's market with a local guide, who will share information about regional ingredients and help you select the best produce for cooking.

✔ **Meal Pairings and Tastings:**

Many cooking classes include meal pairings, often accompanied by **local s** from the **Amalfi Coast vineyards**. Some classes even include a expert to guide you through tasting different s and pairing them with your dishes.

✔ **Post-Class Meals:**

After the cooking experience, enjoy a communal meal where you can savor the dishes you've just prepared. This is often accompanied by fresh **local bread, cheese**, and **desserts** like **limoncello sorbet** or **delicious pastries**.

## 📓 Detailed Description
**A Culinary Immersion on the Amalfi Coast**

**Cooking Classes: Learning the Art of Amalfi Cuisine**

The Amalfi Coast's cuisine is simple yet full of flavor, influenced by its coastal location, fertile land, and centuries of culinary traditions. In the local cooking classes, you'll learn to recreate the **iconic dishes** of the region, such as **Spaghetti alle Vongole**, **Frittura di Paranza** (fried seafood), and the **Amalfi-style limoncello cake**.

Classes typically begin with an introduction to the ingredients, all sourced from local markets or nearby farms, ensuring their freshness and authenticity. Many classes feature hands-on instruction, where you'll learn techniques like kneading dough for **gnocchi** or rolling out **fresh pasta**. By the end of the class, you'll have a deeper appreciation for the flavors and techniques that have made Amalfi Coast cuisine a worldwide sensation.

**Local Markets: A Feast for the Senses**

A visit to the local markets is essential for any food lover traveling along the Amalfi Coast. The colorful stalls are a sensory overload, filled with the scents of **fresh herbs**, **citrus fruits**, and **baked goods**. As you walk through the market, you'll encounter **local farmers**, **cheese makers**, and **fishermen**, each eager to share their knowledge and offer their best products.

During your market tour, you may be able to sample some of the region's most famous foods, including **mozzarella di bufala**, **ricotta**, and **street foods** like **arancini** (fried rice balls) and **pizza margherita** served fresh from a wood-fired oven. For those interested in cooking, the market is the perfect place to source ingredients for your class, giving you a chance to understand the local food culture up close.

### 🔗 Official Websites & Additional Resources

- **Cooking Classes:** Explore local cooking schools and book your culinary experience at [Amalfi Coast Cooking School](#) or [Le Terrazze del Gusto](#) for more details on upcoming classes.
- **Local Markets & Tours:** Check out [Amalfi Coast Market Tours](#) for guided tours of local markets, including information on the best times to visit and what to expect.

Participating in a cooking class and exploring the local markets is the perfect way to connect with the heart and soul of the Amalfi Coast. By learning to prepare iconic dishes and discovering the region's fresh produce, you gain a deeper understanding of the culture and flavors that define this stunning coastline. Whether you're making pasta with a local chef or selecting ingredients for your next meal from the market, these culinary experiences will leave you with lasting memories and a true taste of the Amalfi Coast.

# Chapter 6. Where to Stay: Accommodation Guide

## 6.1 Luxury Hotels & Resorts – Indulge in Amalfi's Finest Stays

**An Unforgettable Experience of Opulence and Scenic Splendor**
The Amalfi Coast is synonymous with unparalleled natural beauty and timeless elegance. Its luxury hotels and resorts provide not just a place to sleep but an immersive experience that combines lavish comfort with breathtaking vistas of the Mediterranean. These properties, often set against dramatic cliffside backdrops, offer world-class amenities, exceptional service, and exquisite design that capture the spirit of the Italian coast. Whether you desire a historic villa steeped in tradition, a modern resort offering cutting-edge luxuries, or a serene retreat complete with private beach access, the Amalfi Coast caters to every discerning traveler.

Featured Properties

**Le Sirenuse – Positano**

- **Location:** Via Cristoforo Colombo, 30, 84017 Positano SA, Italy
- **Contact:** +39 089 875066

- **Website:** sirenuse.it
- **Overview:**

  Le Sirenuse is a legendary luxury hotel perched high above the colorful village of Positano. With its elegant Mediterranean design, this iconic property offers panoramic views of the sparkling Tyrrhenian Sea and the charming town below. Every room is a blend of contemporary comforts and classic Italian style, ensuring an unforgettable stay. Guests can unwind in the infinity pool, indulge in rejuvenating treatments at the spa, and savor world-class cuisine at the Michelin-starred La Sponda Restaurant. Personalized concierge services and exclusive excursions further enhance the luxurious experience.
- **Price Range:** From €600 to €3,000+ per night, varying by room type and season.

### Il San Pietro di Positano – Positano

- **Location:** Via Laurito, 2, 84017 Positano SA, Italy
- **Contact:** +39 089 875022
- **Website:** sanpietro.it
- **Overview:**

  Offering a combination of historical charm and modern luxury, Il San Pietro di Positano provides exclusive access to a private beach and breathtaking sea views. The hotel's suites and villas feature expansive private terraces, perfect for enjoying a sunset over the Mediterranean. Its Michelin-starred restaurant serves innovative local dishes, while amenities such as a beach club and wellness center ensure that guests have an unforgettable and indulgent experience.
- **Price Range:** From €1,200 to €4,500+ per night for premium suites.

### Palazzo Avino – Ravello

- **Location:** Via San Giovanni del Toro, 28, 84010 Ravello SA, Italy
- **Contact:** +39 089 818181
- **Website:** palazzoavino.com
- **Overview:**

  Nestled in the picturesque town of Ravello, Palazzo Avino is housed in a historic 12th-century villa that exudes old-world grandeur. This luxurious resort offers stunning panoramic views of the coastline,

particularly from its renowned rooftop restaurant, Rossellini's, which features gourmet Italian cuisine. The property also boasts an exclusive spa, lavish suites, and personalized services such as helicopter transfers and curated cultural tours.
- **Price Range:** From €700 to €2,800+ per night, with exclusive suites and villas at premium prices.

## Hotel Santa Caterina – Amalfi

- **Location:** SS 163, 84011 Amalfi SA, Italy
- **Contact:** +39 089 871012
- **Website:** [hotelsantacaterina.it](hotelsantacaterina.it)
- **Overview:**
  Set in a historic villa that gracefully marries antiquity with modern luxuries, Hotel Santa Caterina is a jewel on the Amalfi Coast. Guests here enjoy sweeping views of Amalfi Bay, private beach access, and a cliffside pool that offers a refreshing dip in crystal-clear waters. The hotel's restaurant serves an array of fresh, locally sourced Italian dishes, and the attentive concierge service ensures that every guest experiences the best of coastal living.
- **Price Range:** From €800 to €2,200+ per night, depending on room size and amenities.

## Le Agavi – Positano

- **Location:** Via Marconi, 127, 84017 Positano SA, Italy
- **Contact:** +39 089 875067
- **Website:** [leagavi.com](leagavi.com)
- **Overview:**
  Le Agavi is a family-run hotel that epitomizes the charm and warmth of Positano. Perched on the cliffs, it offers mesmerizing views of the Mediterranean along with a private beach, an inviting infinity pool, and an elegant restaurant. The hotel combines modern amenities with traditional Italian hospitality, creating a relaxed yet sophisticated atmosphere ideal for both couples and families.
- **Price Range:** From €450 to €1,800+ per night, with suites boasting unrivaled sea views.

Best Times to Visit

Luxury properties on the Amalfi Coast are open year-round, though peak tourist seasons can affect availability and pricing. The optimal periods to visit are during the spring (April to June) and fall (September to October), when the weather is mild, the crowds are thinner, and the scenic beauty is at its most vibrant.

Services and Amenities

Each of these prestigious properties offers a suite of top-tier services:

- **Concierge and Private Transfers:** Customized itineraries, exclusive tours, and hassle-free transportation.
- **Spa and Wellness Centers:** Full-service spas offering massages, beauty treatments, and wellness programs tailored to rejuvenate the body and soul.
- **Fine Dining Experiences:** On-site Michelin-starred restaurants and gourmet dining options that showcase the best of Mediterranean cuisine.
- **Exclusive Access:** Private beach areas, rooftop pools, and unique cultural excursions that provide an intimate glimpse into the region's heritage.
- **Modern Conveniences:** From high-speed internet and in-room entertainment systems to valet parking and 24-hour room service, these hotels ensure that guests enjoy every modern comfort.

Conclusion

Staying on the Amalfi Coast is not merely about finding a place to sleep—it's about experiencing an unrivaled blend of luxury, history, and natural beauty. Whether you choose the opulence of Le Sirenuse, the exclusive seaside charm of Il San Pietro, or the historic grandeur of Palazzo Avino, each property promises a unique and unforgettable stay. With exceptional service, breathtaking views, and world-class amenities, these luxury hotels and resorts offer the ultimate indulgence for travelers seeking a taste of the Mediterranean dolce vita.

## 6.2 Boutique Hotels & Villas – Intimate Charm and Unique Stays on the Amalfi Coast

For travelers looking to escape the crowds and indulge in a more personalized experience, the boutique hotels and villas along the Amalfi Coast provide an ideal setting. These intimate accommodations, often family-run and steeped in local tradition, offer not only comfort and privacy but also a taste of authentic Mediterranean style. From cliffside retreats with sweeping ocean views to charming hideaways tucked away in quiet villages, these unique properties invite you to experience the Amalfi Coast as if it were your own private paradise.

Featured Properties

### Le Sirenuse Hotel & Villas – Positano

- **Location:** Via Cristoforo Colombo, 30, 84017 Positano SA, Italy
- **Contact:** +39 089 875066
- **Website:** sirenuse.it
- **Overview:**
  Set in the heart of Positano, Le Sirenuse offers an unparalleled blend of luxury and coastal charm. This iconic property features elegantly decorated rooms that combine modern comforts with traditional Mediterranean design elements, such as terracotta floors and sumptuous furnishings. With panoramic views of the sparkling sea and the picturesque village below, guests can relax in style at the infinity pool, rejuvenate at the full-service spa, or savor exquisite dishes at the Michelin-starred La Sponda Restaurant. Personalized concierge services ensure that every aspect of your stay, from private beach transfers to exclusive excursions, is meticulously planned.
- **Price Range:** From €500 to over €2,500 per night, depending on the room category and season.

### Villa Treville – Positano

- **Location:** Via Arienzo, 30, 84017 Positano SA, Italy
- **Contact:** +39 089 875116
- **Website:** villatreville.com
- **Overview:**
  Villa Treville is synonymous with opulence and seclusion, offering private villas that overlook the azure Mediterranean. This luxurious property is designed for those who crave an exclusive escape, with each villa boasting its own infinity pool, spacious terraces, and

impeccable service. Set away from the busy tourist areas, Villa Treville provides a tranquil retreat where guests can enjoy gourmet dining in an intimate setting and partake in bespoke experiences such as private boat tours and wellness treatments.
- **Price Range:** From €800 to over €3,500 per night for exclusive villas and suites.

## Casa Angelina – Praiano

- **Location:** Via Gennaro Capriglione, 147, 84010 Praiano SA, Italy
- **Contact:** +39 089 874101
- **Website:** casangelina.com
- **Overview:**
  Embracing a modern, chic aesthetic, Casa Angelina stands out with its minimalist design and expansive views of the sea. Located in the quieter town of Praiano, this boutique hotel offers a refreshing departure from the bustling Positano scene. Its sleek, contemporary decor is complemented by an outdoor infinity pool and elegantly appointed rooms, all of which invite you to relax in style. Guests enjoy highly personalized service, with offerings such as custom itineraries and private guided tours that showcase the best of the Amalfi Coast's natural and cultural attractions.
- **Price Range:** From €500 to over €1,800 per night, with premium rooms offering panoramic sea views.

## Hotel Onda Verde – Praiano

- **Location:** Via Gennaro Capriglione, 190, 84010 Praiano SA, Italy
- **Contact:** +39 089 874419
- **Website:** hotelondaverde.com
- **Overview:**
  Perched on a cliff in Praiano, Hotel Onda Verde offers a blend of rustic charm and modern comforts. This boutique hotel is renowned for its breathtaking views of the Amalfi Coast, its private rocky beach, and its refined yet relaxed atmosphere. The property features tastefully decorated rooms that evoke the traditional Mediterranean style, and its on-site restaurant serves local seafood and regional specialties. With private tours and boat trips available, guests can fully immerse themselves in the coastal beauty of the region.

- **Price Range:** From €250 to over €1,000 per night.

**Villa Cimbrone – Ravello**

- **Location:** Via Santa Chiara, 26, 84010 Ravello SA, Italy
- **Contact:** +39 089 857459
- **Website:** villacimbrone.com
- **Overview:**
  In the serene town of Ravello, Villa Cimbrone stands as a testament to historical elegance and timeless beauty. Housed in a building dating back to the 12th century, the villa is famous for its lush gardens and the iconic Terrace of Infinity, where sweeping views of the coastline and surrounding mountains create an unforgettable panorama. The atmosphere here is steeped in romance, making it a perfect retreat for couples and anyone seeking a tranquil escape. Special events, such as private concerts and cooking classes, further enrich the experience.
- **Price Range:** From €600 to over €2,000 per night, with the most exclusive suites commanding a premium.

Best Times to Visit

These boutique accommodations are available year-round, though spring (April to June) and fall (September to October) are particularly ideal. During these seasons, the weather is mild, the tourist crowds are thinner, and the natural beauty of the region is at its peak.

Services and Amenities

- **Personalized Concierge:** Every property provides expert concierge services to assist with reservations, tours, and tailored local experiences.
- **Private Tours & Excursions:** Enjoy exclusive access to cultural and outdoor activities, from boat tours along the coast to private vineyard visits.
- **Wellness & Spa Facilities:** Indulge in luxurious spa treatments, yoga sessions, and fitness centers that cater to your well-being.
- **Gourmet Dining:** Savor exceptional Mediterranean and local cuisine at on-site restaurants, often under the guidance of Michelin-star chefs.

- **Exclusive Transportation:** Benefit from services like private chauffeurs, yacht rentals, and helicopter transfers for a seamless travel experience.
- **Beach & Pool Access:** Many properties offer private beach access, infinity pools, and sun loungers, ensuring you can relax in style.

Conclusion

Choosing a boutique hotel or villa on the Amalfi Coast is more than just booking a room—it's about embracing a lifestyle that is as unique as it is luxurious. These intimate properties offer the perfect combination of modern comforts, personalized service, and authentic local charm. Whether you're captivated by the dramatic views at Le Sirenuse, the secluded tranquility of Villa Treville, the modern sophistication of Casa Angelina, the rustic elegance of Hotel Onda Verde, or the historic allure of Villa Cimbrone, your stay on the Amalfi Coast will be nothing short of extraordinary. Indulge in the intimate luxury and timeless beauty of these exquisite accommodations for an unforgettable Mediterranean escape.

## 6.3 Budget-Friendly Stays & B&Bs – Affordable Charm on the Amalfi Coast

While the Amalfi Coast is often associated with luxury, there are plenty of **budget-friendly stays and bed and breakfasts (B&Bs)** that allow travelers to experience this stunning destination without breaking the bank. These accommodations offer a perfect blend of local charm, comfort, and great value for money. With some of the best locations near key towns and attractions, these stays are ideal for those looking to enjoy the Amalfi Coast on a budget, without sacrificing the beauty and authenticity of the region.

### 📍 Location & Address

1. **La Caravella - B&B – Amalfi**

    - **Address:** Via Casa Mannini, 5, 84011 Amalfi SA, Italy
    - **Contact:** +39 089 871570

- **Website:** www.bblacaravella.com
2. **Villa Lara – Amalfi**

    - **Address:** Via Mauro Comite, 35, 84011 Amalfi SA, Italy
    - **Contact:** +39 089 871777
    - **Website:** www.villalara.com
3. **B&B Il Rifugio – Positano**

    - **Address:** Via Pasitea, 312, 84017 Positano SA, Italy
    - **Contact:** +39 089 875280
    - **Website:** www.bbrifugio.com
4. **La Zagara B&B – Praiano**

    - **Address:** Via Gennaro Capriglione, 72, 84010 Praiano SA, Italy
    - **Contact:** +39 089 874504
    - **Website:** www.lazagarabedandbreakfast.com
5. **B&B Casa Nilde – Ravello**

    - **Address:** Via San Francesco, 3, 84010 Ravello SA, Italy
    - **Contact:** +39 089 857681
    - **Website:** www.casnilde.com

## 💰 Price Range

The price for budget-friendly stays and B&Bs on the Amalfi Coast is generally more affordable compared to luxury hotels and resorts, making them a great choice for travelers on a budget. Here's an approximate price range:

1. **La Caravella – Amalfi**

    - **Price Range:** From €80 to €160 per night, depending on the season and room type.
2. **Villa Lara – Amalfi**

    - **Price Range:** From €90 to €180 per night, depending on the room and view.
3. **B&B Il Rifugio – Positano**

- **Price Range:** From €100 to €190 per night, with basic rooms priced lower and sea-view rooms or suites at a premium.

4. **La Zagara B&B – Praiano**

    - **Price Range:** From €70 to €150 per night, depending on the room type and season.

5. **B&B Casa Nilde – Ravello**

    - **Price Range:** From €85 to €170 per night, with rooms offering garden or sea views at a higher price point.

## 🌟 Key Features & Highlights

### La Caravella – Amalfi

- **Central Location:** Located in the heart of Amalfi, just a short walk from the main square, the beach, and key attractions like the **Cathedral of Amalfi**.
- **Cozy Rooms:** Simple, comfortable rooms with modern amenities, providing a peaceful retreat after a day of sightseeing.
- **Charming Decor:** A rustic yet contemporary design that blends perfectly with the Mediterranean surroundings.
- **Delicious Breakfast:** Fresh local produce is used in the daily breakfast, served on the terrace with views of the town.
- **Visitor Services:** Free Wi-Fi, luggage storage, airport transfers (for an additional charge), and helpful staff to arrange local tours and excursions.

### Villa Lara – Amalfi

- **Panoramic Views:** Situated high on the cliffs, Villa Lara offers breathtaking views over Amalfi and the Mediterranean Sea.
- **Tranquil Atmosphere:** A family-run B&B with a homely feel and exceptional hospitality, offering a relaxing escape from the bustling towns.

- **Comfortable Rooms:** Bright and airy rooms with elegant decor, including air conditioning, minibars, and flat-screen TVs.
- **Terrace Garden:** Guests can enjoy a peaceful breakfast in the garden while taking in panoramic views.
- **Visitor Services:** Complimentary breakfast, free Wi-Fi, room service, and assistance with booking tours and activities.

### B&B Il Rifugio – Positano

- **Close to the Beach:** Just a short walk from the iconic **Spiaggia Grande**, Il Rifugio offers easy access to Positano's beaches and vibrant town center.
- **Simple & Modern Rooms:** Rooms are cozy, with a minimalist design, perfect for those who want comfort without unnecessary frills.
- **Sea-View Terrace:** Some rooms have balconies with spectacular views of Positano's colorful buildings and the coastline.
- **Welcoming Hosts:** Known for its warm and friendly hosts who are always happy to provide recommendations for local restaurants and activities.
- **Visitor Services:** Free breakfast, air conditioning, daily housekeeping, and free Wi-Fi.

### La Zagara B&B – Praiano

- **Charming Location:** Nestled in the village of Praiano, this B&B offers a quiet and more local experience compared to the busier towns of Positano and Amalfi.
- **Breathtaking Views:** Rooms offer panoramic views of the Mediterranean and the famous **Li Galli islands**, a prime spot for a peaceful retreat.
- **Comfortable & Cozy:** Rooms come with air conditioning, private bathrooms, and all the essentials for a comfortable stay.
- **Vibrant Garden:** The property features a garden full of fragrant lemon and orange trees, perfect for relaxing after a day of sightseeing.
- **Visitor Services:** Free Wi-Fi, daily breakfast served in the garden, private transfers, and tips on the best local hikes and attractions.

### B&B Casa Nilde – Ravello

- **Historic Charm:** Located in the hilltop town of Ravello, Casa Nilde is housed in a charming building that reflects the historical ambiance of the region.
- **Elegant Rooms:** The rooms are simple yet elegant, offering great comfort with antique furniture and modern amenities like free Wi-Fi, flat-screen TVs, and minibars.
- **Stunning Views:** Rooms offer views over Ravello's terraced hills, gardens, and the surrounding coastline.
- **Peaceful Surroundings:** A tranquil B&B perfect for those looking to escape the tourist crowds while being close to Ravello's cultural treasures.
- **Visitor Services:** Daily breakfast, free Wi-Fi, luggage storage, concierge services, and assistance with booking tours and excursions in the area.

### Opening Hours & Best Time to Visit

- **La Caravella – Amalfi**
  Open year-round, with the peak season being from **April to October**, when the weather is perfect for outdoor activities and exploring Amalfi. Off-season months may see lower rates.

- **Villa Lara – Amalfi**
  Open year-round, with spring and fall offering a quieter, more relaxed atmosphere with fewer tourists, and pleasant weather for sightseeing.

- **B&B Il Rifugio – Positano**
  Open year-round, though it's best to visit during **spring and fall** for more affordable rates and a more relaxed atmosphere compared to the busy summer months.

- **La Zagara B&B – Praiano**
  Open year-round, with the best time to visit in **April to June** or **September to October** when the weather is mild and the crowds are smaller.

- **B&B Casa Nilde – Ravello**
  Open year-round, with **April to June** and **September to October**

being the best times to visit Ravello for mild weather and fewer tourists.

### 🛠 Visitor Services

- **Complimentary Breakfast:** Most of the budget B&Bs and stays offer a simple yet delicious continental or Mediterranean-style breakfast with fresh local produce.
- **Free Wi-Fi:** All B&Bs offer free Wi-Fi to stay connected during your stay.
- **Guided Tours & Excursions:** Some B&Bs can help arrange local tours, hiking trips, and excursions, such as visits to **Pompeii**, **Herculaneum**, and **Vesuvius**.
- **Transfers & Shuttle Services:** Many of the B&Bs offer affordable transfers from the airport, as well as shuttles to nearby beaches and attractions.
- **Luggage Storage & Room Service:** Guests can request luggage storage before check-in or after check-out, and some properties offer room service for added convenience.

For travelers seeking a more affordable option without compromising the beauty of the **Amalfi Coast**, these **budget-friendly stays and B&Bs** provide the perfect balance of value, comfort, and convenience. With their welcoming atmospheres, excellent locations, and personalized service, these properties ensure that even those on a tighter budget can enjoy the charms of this stunning destination. Whether you choose to stay in **Amalfi**, **Positano**, **Praiano**, or **Ravello**, these budget-friendly accommodations offer an unforgettable experience that allows you to enjoy all the Amalfi Coast has to offer without overspending.

## 6.4 Best Areas to Stay on the Amalfi Coast

The Amalfi Coast is a diverse and captivating region, and where you stay can significantly impact your experience. Whether you're looking for a charming town filled with history, a tranquil hideaway with stunning views, or a lively beachside escape, there's an area on the Amalfi Coast for every kind of traveler. Here's a guide to some of the best areas to stay, including price ranges, key features, and accommodation options for all budgets.

### 1. Amalfi – The Heart of the Coast

📍 **Location & Address**

- **Town:** Amalfi
- **Address:** Amalfi, 84011, Salerno, Italy

💰 **Price Range**

- **Luxury Hotels:** From €200 to €500+ per night.
- **Mid-Range Hotels:** From €100 to €200 per night.
- **Budget-Friendly Accommodations:** From €70 to €150 per night.

✨ **Key Features**

- **Central Hub:** Amalfi is one of the most iconic towns on the coast, offering a lively yet relaxed atmosphere with plenty of restaurants, shops, and historic landmarks like the **Amalfi Cathedral**.
- **Beautiful Beaches:** Amalfi has a mix of public and private beaches, perfect for lounging or swimming.
- **Historic Charm:** The town is home to beautiful piazzas, charming streets, and historic churches that showcase its cultural importance as a medieval maritime republic.
- **Accessibility:** Well-connected by buses and ferries to other coastal towns like Positano, Ravello, and Sorrento.

🏛 **Visitor Services**

- **Transportation:** Access to buses, ferries, and taxis.
- **Local Shops:** Plenty of boutiques, artisanal shops, and souvenir stores.
- **Restaurants & Cafés:** A range of dining options from traditional seafood restaurants to trendy cafés.
- **Tourist Information Centers:** Available for booking tours, excursions, and providing information on nearby attractions.

🌐 **Website:**

Visit Amalfi

### 2. Positano – A Picturesque Cliffside Escape

📍 **Location & Address**

- **Town:** Positano
- **Address:** Positano, 84017, Salerno, Italy

💰 **Price Range**

- **Luxury Hotels:** From €400 to €800+ per night.
- **Mid-Range Hotels:** From €200 to €400 per night.
- **Budget-Friendly Accommodations:** From €100 to €250 per night.

✨ **Key Features**

- **Stunning Views:** Positano is famed for its colorful hillside houses that cascade down to the Mediterranean Sea, offering breathtaking views from nearly every vantage point.
- **Vibrant Atmosphere:** Known for its upscale boutiques, fine dining, and fashionable vibe, it attracts celebrities and honeymooners alike.
- **Beaches & Sunsets:** The town is home to **Spiaggia Grande**, a beautiful pebble beach perfect for relaxing or enjoying boat tours.
- **Romantic Vibe:** Its winding streets and narrow alleys are perfect for a romantic evening stroll.

🏛 **Visitor Services**

- **Beach Access:** Access to **Spiaggia Grande** beach, with plenty of lounges, bars, and water sports available.
- **Public Transport:** Well-connected by bus and ferry to other Amalfi Coast towns.
- **Boat Rentals:** Opportunities to rent boats or take guided tours around the coast.
- **Wellness Centers & Spas:** Several luxury hotels feature on-site spas for relaxation.

🌐 **Website:**

[Visit Positano](#)

### 3. Ravello – A Peaceful Hilltop Retreat

#### 📍 Location & Address

- **Town:** Ravello
- **Address:** Ravello, 84010, Salerno, Italy

#### 💰 Price Range

- **Luxury Hotels:** From €250 to €600+ per night.
- **Mid-Range Hotels:** From €150 to €250 per night.
- **Budget-Friendly Accommodations:** From €100 to €200 per night.

#### ✹ Key Features

- **Panoramic Views:** Ravello is perched high above the coast, offering some of the best panoramic views on the entire Amalfi Coast. Its vantage point provides sweeping vistas of the Mediterranean and surrounding hills.
- **Cultural Heritage:** Known for its cultural festivals, Ravello is a UNESCO World Heritage site filled with art galleries, historical buildings, and stunning gardens, including the famous **Villa Rufolo** and **Villa Cimbrone**.
- **Tranquil Atmosphere:** Unlike Positano or Amalfi, Ravello is quieter, making it ideal for those seeking peace and relaxation.
- **Great for Hiking:** The surrounding mountains offer numerous hiking trails with spectacular views.

#### 🏛 Visitor Services

- **Cultural Attractions:** Museums, galleries, and historic villas to explore.
- **Transport Connections:** Accessible via bus from Amalfi and other coastal towns.
- **Local Markets:** Great markets for artisan crafts and local products.
- **Wellness and Yoga:** Many boutique hotels offer yoga retreats and wellness services.

🌐 **Website:**

Visit Ravello

### 4. Praiano – A Hidden Gem Between Positano and Amalfi

📍 **Location & Address**

- **Town:** Praiano
- **Address:** Praiano, 84010, Salerno, Italy

💰 **Price Range**

- **Luxury Hotels:** From €150 to €400 per night.
- **Mid-Range Hotels:** From €100 to €200 per night.
- **Budget-Friendly Accommodations:** From €70 to €150 per night.

✨ **Key Features**

- **Secluded Escape:** Praiano is less touristy than Positano and Amalfi, making it a quieter destination with a more authentic vibe.
- **Stunning Sunsets:** Praiano is known for its panoramic sea views and especially its sunsets, which can be enjoyed from the cliffside restaurants or your private terrace.
- **Charming Beaches:** The town is home to two pebbled beaches, **Marina di Praia** and **La Gavitella**, both offering pristine waters and quiet, relaxing atmospheres.
- **Authentic Amalfi Coast Experience:** With fewer crowds, it offers a more laid-back, local experience with traditional Mediterranean charm.

🏛 **Visitor Services**

- **Shuttle Services:** Shuttle buses are available to take you to nearby towns like Positano and Amalfi.
- **Boat Excursions:** Opportunities to book boat tours or private boat rentals to explore the coastline.
- **Restaurants & Cafés:** Authentic Italian eateries offering delicious seafood and local specialties.
- **Hiking Routes:** Several well-maintained trails are perfect for those looking to hike and explore the surrounding hills.

🌐 **Website:**

Visit Praiano


### 5. Maiori & Minori – Tranquil Towns with Less Crowds

📍 **Location & Address**

- **Town:** Maiori & Minori
- **Address:** Maiori and Minori, 84010, Salerno, Italy

💰 **Price Range**

- **Luxury Hotels:** From €120 to €300 per night.
- **Mid-Range Hotels:** From €80 to €150 per night.
- **Budget-Friendly Accommodations:** From €50 to €100 per night.

🌟 **Key Features**

- **Relaxed Atmosphere:** Maiori and Minori offer a slower pace of life compared to the more bustling towns of the Amalfi Coast, making them ideal for families or those looking for a more peaceful retreat.
- **Long Beaches:** The two towns have some of the longest and most accessible beaches on the Amalfi Coast, perfect for swimming and sunbathing.
- **Authentic Italian Experience:** These towns offer a more authentic Italian coastal experience, with local markets, bakeries, and cafés that give a glimpse into everyday life on the coast.
- **Convenient Location:** Well-connected by ferry and bus to Amalfi, Ravello, and other coastal towns.

🛎️ **Visitor Services**

- **Shuttle Services:** Frequent connections by bus to Amalfi, Ravello, and other nearby towns.
- **Restaurants & Cafés:** Many seaside cafés and pizzerias offer fresh seafood and local Amalfi Coast dishes.
- **Beach Amenities:** Plenty of beach loungers, umbrellas, and beachfront cafés for added comfort.

- **Local Markets:** Both towns host regular markets with fresh produce and local artisan goods.

🌐 **Website:**

[Visit Maiori & Minori](#)

Each area along the Amalfi Coast has its unique charm and appeal, whether you're seeking the bustling beauty of Positano, the historical richness of Ravello, or the tranquil beauty of Praiano. From luxury resorts to budget-friendly stays, these towns offer something for every type of traveler. Consider what suits your style, whether it's a cultural escape, a romantic retreat, or a family-friendly adventure, and choose the perfect base for your Amalfi Coast experience.

# Chapter 7. Food & Drink: Culinary Guide

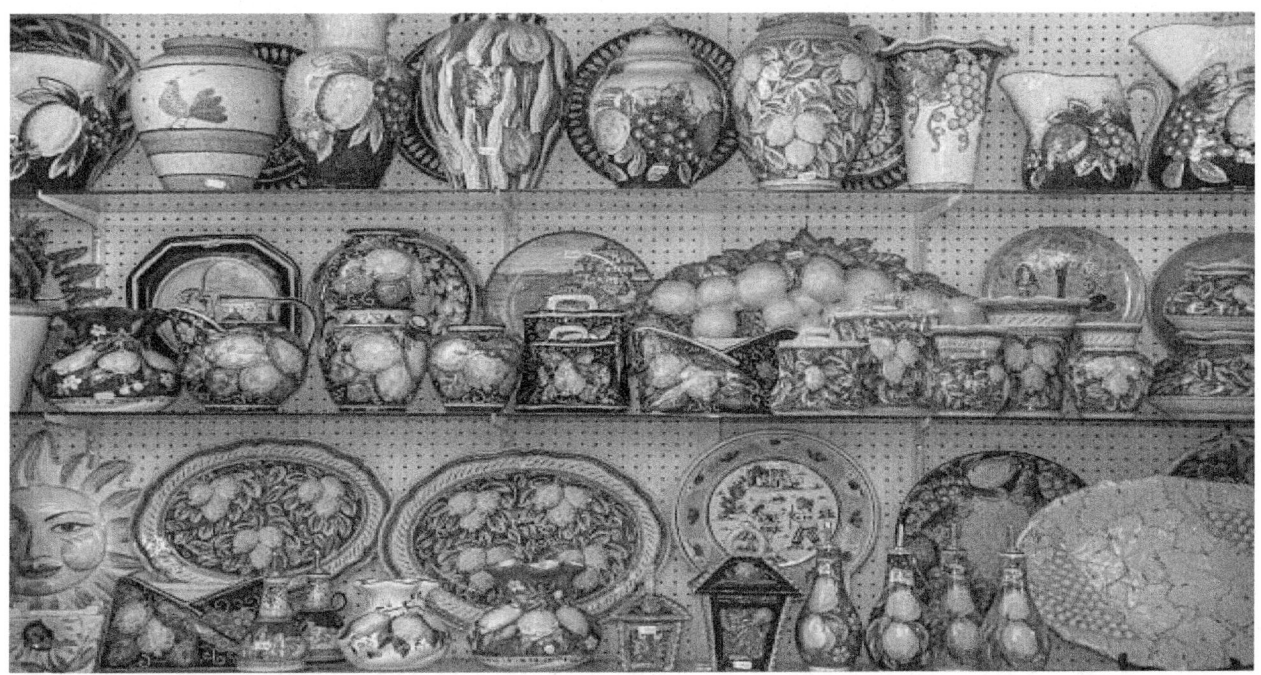

## 6.1 Must-Try New Mexican Dishes: A Culinary Journey Through Tradition and Flavor

New Mexico's cuisine is a vibrant tapestry woven from centuries of Native American, Spanish, and Anglo influences. Its food is deeply connected to the region's history, climate, and the agricultural traditions that have flourished over generations. Whether you're enjoying the bold, spicy kick of green chile, savoring the comforting warmth of homemade tamales, or indulging in the sweet crunch of biscochitos, every dish tells a story of heritage and passion. Here's an expanded guide to some of the iconic dishes that define New Mexican culinary culture, along with insights into their origins and ways to enjoy them.

Green Chile: The Heartbeat of New Mexican Flavor

**A Storied Staple**

Green chile is synonymous with New Mexican cuisine. Cultivated locally, varieties like Anaheim, Hatch, and Poblano contribute to an unmistakable flavor profile that is both smoky and spicy. Introduced by Spanish settlers in the 16th century, green chile quickly became an indispensable ingredient, infusing local dishes with a distinctive tang and heat that vary from mild to fiery.

**How It's Enjoyed**

- **Roasted Green Chile:** Often prepared by roasting over an open flame, then peeling the skin off to reveal the tender, flavorful flesh. This version is typically added to salsas, soups, and stews for an extra layer of complexity.
- **Green Chile Stew:** A hearty, comforting dish where pork, potatoes, and onions are simmered with roasted green chile. Served over a bed of rice or with warm tortillas, it's a perfect meal to combat cooler desert evenings.
- **Green Chile Cheeseburger:** A local twist on a classic favorite, where a succulent burger is crowned with roasted green chile and melted cheese, offering a delightful burst of flavor with every bite.

**Key Characteristics**

Green chile brings together an earthy, smoky depth with a vibrant heat, making it a versatile addition that enhances everything from simple breakfasts to elaborate dinners.

Tamales: A Timeless Tradition

**Historical Roots and Cultural Significance**

Tamales are a beloved dish in New Mexico, steeped in both Native American and Spanish culinary traditions. Made from corn masa filled with ingredients such as savory meats, cheeses, or even spicy chile, tamales are wrapped in corn husks and steamed to perfection. This dish has its origins in ancient Aztec and Pueblo cultures, where tamales were an essential part of ceremonial feasts. The Spanish introduced the practice of wrapping and steaming, transforming tamales into the cherished comfort food they are today.

**Serving Styles**

- **Christmas Tamales:** A communal favorite during the holiday season, where families gather to prepare and share tamales, celebrating tradition and togetherness.

- **Accompaniments:** Typically served with vibrant red or green chile sauces, or even a dollop of sour cream, tamales offer a deliciously warm and hearty flavor that's both satisfying and nostalgic.

### Versatility and Texture
The beauty of tamales lies in their versatility—the filling options are nearly endless, and the soft masa contrasts beautifully with the texture of the corn husk, creating a delightful mouthfeel that's both tender and hearty.

Biscochitos: The Official Taste of New Mexico

### Cultural and Culinary Heritage
Biscochitos, the official state cookie of New Mexico, are a festive treat that carries deep historical significance. With roots tracing back to early Spanish settlers, these crisp cookies are traditionally flavored with anise and dusted with cinnamon sugar. Biscochitos were once a staple at weddings, religious ceremonies, and festive gatherings, symbolizing celebration and joy.

### How They're Enjoyed

- **At Celebrations:** Biscochitos are most commonly served during Christmas and New Year's, though their delightful taste makes them a year-round favorite.
- **As a Snack:** These cookies pair perfectly with a cup of hot cocoa or coffee, providing a sweet yet spiced complement to any meal.

### Key Attributes
With a perfectly balanced mix of anise, cinnamon, and sugar, biscochitos offer a crunchy, satisfying bite that encapsulates the warmth and spirit of New Mexican festivities.

Other Culinary Gems of New Mexico

### Chiles Rellenos

- **Description:** This dish features roasted peppers, usually Poblano or Anaheim, stuffed with cheese, meat, or beans, then battered and fried to a golden crisp. Often served with a side of fresh salsa and rice, chiles rellenos are a hearty, savory option that showcases the region's love for bold flavors.

- **Key Characteristics:** Smoky, cheesy, and rich in flavor, this dish is a perfect example of New Mexico's fusion of culinary influences.

**Sopaipillas**

- **Description:** These light, puffy fried dough treats are a popular accompaniment to many New Mexican meals. Often drizzled with honey or served alongside savory stews, sopaipillas provide a delightful contrast to the spiciness of chile-based dishes.
- **Key Characteristics:** Crispy on the outside and soft on the inside, they are a versatile side that works equally well as a dessert or a savory snack.

**Posole**

- **Description:** A traditional stew made with hominy corn and tender chunks of pork or chicken, posole is flavored with red or green chile and is especially popular during winter holidays and festivals.
- **Key Characteristics:** This dish is known for its rich, warming flavor and subtle spicy kick, making it a comforting choice on chilly days.

Summary

New Mexico's culinary landscape is a vibrant celebration of its diverse cultural heritage. The bold, smoky flavors of green chile, the comforting warmth of tamales, and the crisp sweetness of biscochitos exemplify the state's unique approach to food—a blend of tradition, innovation, and deep-rooted history. Each dish offers a window into the region's past, from ancient Native American practices to the culinary influences brought by Spanish settlers. Whether you're dining at a family-run trattoria, savoring street food at a local festival, or enjoying a meal with friends and family, New Mexican cuisine provides a rich, flavorful experience that is truly one-of-a-kind. Enjoying these iconic dishes is not just about feeding the body, but also about nourishing the soul with the timeless tastes and stories of New Mexico.

## 6.2 Boutique Hotels & Villas – Intimate Charm and Unique Stays on the Amalfi Coast

For those travelers who prefer a more personalized and exclusive experience, the Amalfi Coast boasts an array of boutique hotels and villas that radiate local charm and refined elegance. These intimate accommodations—often family-run—offer a cozy, home-like atmosphere combined with luxurious amenities and unforgettable views of the Mediterranean. Whether you're seeking a cliffside hideaway, a quaint villa in a quiet village, or a stylish boutique hotel in the heart of the coast, these properties provide a unique blend of comfort, privacy, and authentic Italian character.

Experience the Essence of the Amalfi Coast

Staying at a boutique hotel or villa on the Amalfi Coast is more than just booking a room—it's about immersing yourself in a world where history, art, and nature converge. Many of these properties are housed in centuries-old buildings that have been lovingly restored, preserving traditional architecture while incorporating modern conveniences. The interiors are often adorned with local artwork, antique furnishings, and bespoke details that tell the story of the region's rich cultural heritage. Imagine waking up to panoramic vistas of sparkling blue waters, enjoying a leisurely breakfast on a sun-drenched terrace, and spending your afternoons exploring charming coastal towns—all from the comfort of an elegantly designed retreat.

Selected Properties

**Le Sirenuse Hotel & Villas – Positano**

- **Location:** Via Cristoforo Colombo, 30, 84017 Positano SA, Italy
- **Overview:** Nestled high above Positano, Le Sirenuse is a renowned establishment that epitomizes luxury on the Amalfi Coast. With its breathtaking cliffside position, every room offers sweeping views of the vibrant town and the Mediterranean Sea below.
- **Key Features:**
    - Exquisite Mediterranean design blending classic and contemporary elements
    - Private villas and suites with exclusive terraces and infinity pools
    - Michelin-starred dining at La Sponda, where candlelit meals enhance the romantic ambiance
    - Personalized concierge services, private beach access, and curated excursions for a tailored guest experience

- **Experience:** Whether enjoying a sunset cocktail on the terrace or a private dinner in a secluded villa, Le Sirenuse delivers an immersive experience steeped in elegance and natural beauty.

**Villa Treville – Positano**

- **Location:** Via Arienzo, 30, 84017 Positano SA, Italy
- **Overview:** Villa Treville transforms a former estate into an exclusive boutique hotel, offering guests privacy and a sense of historical grandeur. Its unique setting away from the busiest tourist areas makes it an ideal retreat for discerning travelers seeking tranquility and sophistication.
- **Key Features:**
    - Luxurious private villas with infinity pools and panoramic sea views
    - A secluded ambiance that ensures complete privacy and relaxation
    - Gourmet dining experiences featuring locally inspired cuisine
    - Exclusive access to private beach areas and personalized boat tours
- **Experience:** At Villa Treville, every detail is curated to create a luxurious escape, whether you're lounging by the infinity pool, enjoying a candlelit dinner, or exploring the hidden coves of Positano by boat.

**Casa Angelina – Praiano**

- **Location:** Via Gennaro Capriglione, 147, 84010 Praiano SA, Italy
- **Overview:** Casa Angelina is a modern boutique hotel that stands out for its sleek, minimalist design and awe-inspiring views of the Mediterranean. Located in the peaceful town of Praiano, it offers an idyllic escape from the more crowded areas of the coast.
- **Key Features:**
    - Contemporary design with clean lines and elegant décor
    - Expansive terraces that offer uninterrupted views of the sea and coastline
    - An infinity pool and wellness center for rejuvenation
    - Personalized service with a focus on sustainable practices and local culinary delights

- **Experience:** Guests at Casa Angelina can indulge in refined dining, relax in a serene spa, and enjoy the sophisticated ambiance that blends modern luxury with the timeless allure of the Amalfi Coast.

**Hotel Onda Verde – Praiano**

- **Location:** Via Gennaro Capriglione, 190, 84010 Praiano SA, Italy
- **Overview:** Hotel Onda Verde offers a blend of rustic charm and modern comfort, set against the dramatic backdrop of Praiano's rugged coastline. Its intimate setting and casual elegance provide the perfect environment to relax and enjoy the natural beauty of the region.
- **Key Features:**
    - Stunning cliffside location with spectacular sea views
    - Cozy, traditionally styled rooms paired with contemporary amenities
    - Exclusive access to a private rocky beach and outdoor dining areas
    - On-site dining featuring fresh, locally sourced seafood and Mediterranean specialties
- **Experience:** Whether you're dining al fresco with a view or unwinding in the privacy of your room, Hotel Onda Verde offers a warm and inviting retreat that captures the essence of the Amalfi lifestyle.

**Villa Cimbrone – Ravello**

- **Location:** Via Santa Chiara, 26, 84010 Ravello SA, Italy
- **Overview:** Perched in the historic town of Ravello, Villa Cimbrone is a symbol of elegance and timeless beauty. Its famous Terrace of Infinity is one of the most celebrated viewpoints in Italy, offering sweeping vistas of the coastline and the surrounding mountains.
- **Key Features:**
    - Historic architecture dating back to the 12th century, exuding old-world charm
    - Lush, meticulously maintained gardens that enhance the villa's romantic atmosphere
    - Private suites and exclusive villas designed for an intimate, luxury stay

- - Facilities for hosting private events, including weddings and cultural gatherings
- **Experience:** Villa Cimbrone provides a unique blend of history, art, and natural beauty. Whether exploring the expansive gardens, enjoying a gourmet meal with a view, or simply relaxing on the terrace, guests experience a journey back in time with the comforts of modern luxury.

Summary

Boutique hotels and villas along the Amalfi Coast offer more than just luxurious accommodations—they provide an immersive experience that reflects the region's unique blend of history, culture, and natural beauty. These intimate retreats allow you to escape the crowds and enjoy personalized service, whether you're savoring a Michelin-starred meal, relaxing in a private villa, or exploring the scenic coastline in complete comfort. For travelers seeking an authentic and exclusive stay on the Amalfi Coast, these properties deliver an unforgettable fusion of local charm and high-end luxury.

## 7.3 Street Food & Local Markets

The Amalfi Coast is not just known for its elegant restaurants and luxurious dining experiences; it also boasts an incredible selection of **street food** and **local markets** that give you a taste of the region's authentic flavors and vibrant culture. Whether you're strolling through the charming streets of Positano, Amalfi, or Ravello, you'll find an array of local snacks, fresh produce, and traditional treats that embody the soul of the Amalfi Coast.

### Street Food on the Amalfi Coast

The Amalfi Coast's **street food scene** is a delightful mix of fresh, locally sourced ingredients, simple yet flavorful preparations, and age-old recipes passed down through generations. It's the perfect way to experience the region's culinary heritage while on the go.

### 1. Pizza Margherita

**Location:** Available throughout the Amalfi Coast
**Price:** €5–€10

**Description:** Perhaps Italy's most famous dish, **Pizza Margherita** is a must-try while visiting the Amalfi Coast. This classic pizza is topped with a simple combination of tomato, mozzarella, and fresh basil, symbolizing the colors of the Italian flag. The Amalfi Coast's pizza is often served by street vendors in charming, hole-in-the-wall eateries or food stalls in bustling towns like Positano or Amalfi. With its crispy thin crust and perfectly melted cheese, it's the ideal snack for a midday break or a casual dinner on the go.

## 2. Frittura di Paranza (Fried Seafood)

**Location:** Coastal towns such as Positano, Amalfi, and Praiano
**Price:** €6–€12

**Description: Frittura di Paranza** refers to a mix of fresh, local seafood that is lightly battered and fried to perfection. Typically served in paper cones, this street food is the perfect way to enjoy the region's abundance of seafood while wandering the streets or enjoying the beach. You can find vendors serving up squid, anchovies, small fish, and shrimp, all crispy and golden on the outside, with tender, juicy flesh on the inside. Paired with a squeeze of lemon and a side of dipping sauce, it's a treat you can't miss.

## 3. Delizia al Limone (Lemon Delight)

**Location:** Amalfi, Ravello, Positano
**Price:** €3–€6

**Description:** Made with the Amalfi Coast's famous lemons, **Delizia al Limone** is a small, creamy dessert that combines a delicate sponge cake with a tangy lemon filling and a layer of lemon icing. This delightful treat is a must-try for anyone visiting the region and is often sold in bakeries, pastry shops, and from street vendors throughout the coast. Its refreshing, citrusy taste is perfect for cooling off after a warm day spent exploring.

## 4. Crocche di Patate (Potato Croquettes)

**Location:** Available in towns like Amalfi, Positano, and Ravello
**Price:** €2–€5

**Description:** These delicious golden croquettes are made with mashed potatoes, cheese, and spices, then deep-fried until crispy and golden. Often enjoyed as a snack or appetizer, **Crocche di Patate** can be found at local food stalls or even served in small street-side eateries. They are light, flavorful, and a true comfort food of the region, perfect for a midday snack or an accompaniment to a cold drink.

### 5. Panino con Porchetta (Porchetta Sandwich)

**Location:** Throughout the Amalfi Coast, especially in smaller towns
**Price:** €5–€8
**Description:** The **Panino con Porchetta** is a popular sandwich made with slow-roasted, tender pork, seasoned with herbs, garlic, and fennel. Often served on fresh, crusty bread and accompanied by a touch of olive oil and arugula, it's the perfect street food option for a quick and hearty meal. This dish is particularly popular in markets and food stalls and is an excellent way to experience local flavors while exploring the towns.

### Local Markets on the Amalfi Coast

The local markets on the Amalfi Coast are an essential part of its culinary scene. They provide an opportunity to taste the freshest produce, sample artisanal products, and take home local delicacies that you might not find anywhere else. Visiting these markets offers not only a gastronomic adventure but also a cultural experience, allowing you to see the heart of the region's food traditions and artisanal craftsmanship.

### 1. Amalfi Market (Mercato di Amalfi)

**Location:** Piazza del Duomo, Amalfi
**Opening Hours:** Monday to Saturday, 8:00 AM – 2:00 PM
**Key Features:**

- Fresh produce including tomatoes, lemons, and olives
- Artisanal cheeses and meats
- Local honey and jams
- Handcrafted products from local artisans

**Description:** The **Amalfi Market** is one of the most popular and vibrant markets on the coast. Held in the heart of Amalfi, it's a great place to pick up the region's famous fresh ingredients, such as juicy lemons, ripe tomatoes, and the ever-popular anchovies. The market also sells a variety of handmade goods, from locally made ceramics to traditional pasta. For foodies, it's an opportunity to explore the region's produce and bring home some of the best ingredients to recreate Amalfi Coast recipes.

## 2. Positano Market (Mercato di Positano)

**Location:** Piazza dei Mulini, Positano
**Opening Hours:** Tuesday to Sunday, 8:00 AM – 1:00 PM
**Key Features:**

- Local seafood and cured meats
- Fresh fruits and vegetables
- Olive oils and balsamic vinegars
- Freshly baked bread

**Description:** The **Positano Market** is smaller but equally charming. Located near the center of Positano, the market features fresh seasonal produce and the best ingredients the Amalfi Coast has to offer. If you're looking for freshly caught fish or a selection of cured meats, this is the place to be. You'll also find a variety of homemade pastries and delicious Italian bread, perfect for enjoying a fresh sandwich or snack as you explore the town.

## 3. Ravello Market (Mercato di Ravello)

**Location:** Piazza del Vescovado, Ravello
**Opening Hours:** Monday to Saturday, 9:00 AM – 2:00 PM
**Key Features:**

- Fresh herbs, fruits, and vegetables
- Local cheeses, including mozzarella and ricotta
- Handcrafted ceramic goods
- Homemade liqueurs

**Description:** Ravello's market offers a more serene and relaxed atmosphere compared to the busier markets of Amalfi or Positano, but it is no less charming. Here, you'll find an array of fresh fruits, vegetables, and local delicacies, including mozzarella di bufala, ricotta, and other cheeses produced in the area. The market also offers a selection of homemade **limoncello** and **grappa**, perfect for taking home a taste of the coast.

### 4. Praiano Farmers Market

**Location:** Via G. Marconi, Praiano
**Opening Hours:** Thursdays, 9:00 AM – 1:00 PM
**Key Features:**

- Fresh, seasonal local produce
- Organic offerings from surrounding farms
- Local s and olive oils

**Description:** The **Praiano Farmers Market** is a smaller, more intimate market compared to the others on the coast but offers a wonderful selection of local organic produce. This market is a great place to find seasonal fruits and vegetables, as well as hand-picked herbs and spices. You'll also discover homemade preserves and jars of Amalfi Coast olive oils, perfect for those looking to take home authentic local flavors.

The Amalfi Coast offers much more than luxurious dining options; it's a place where street food and local markets bring the region's culinary traditions to life. From the simplicity of **Pizza Margherita** enjoyed on a cliffside to the richness of fresh seafood fried on the spot, street food on the Amalfi Coast is an experience not to be missed. Local markets offer a glimpse into the authentic flavors and lifestyle of this iconic region, where every visit to a stall or vendor opens the door to new, unforgettable tastes.

By exploring the local food scene, you'll not only enjoy delicious meals but also discover the soul of the Amalfi Coast, one bite at a time.

# Chapter 8. Travel Tips & Essentials

## 8.1 Packing Guide for the Amalfi Coast

Traveling to the Amalfi Coast—a region famous for its cliffside villages, dramatic seascapes, and irresistible Mediterranean charm—requires careful preparation. Whether you're planning to trek along the legendary Path of the Gods, relax on a secluded beach, or enjoy a sumptuous seafood dinner at a cliffside eatery, packing smartly will ensure your journey is both comfortable and unforgettable. Below is an expanded, detailed guide to help you pack all the essentials, along with a few bonus items that can enhance your Amalfi Coast adventure.

1. Clothing Essentials

**Adaptable Apparel for Changing Conditions**
 The Amalfi Coast enjoys a Mediterranean climate characterized by hot, dry summers and mild, occasionally rainy winters. To comfortably navigate these seasonal shifts, pack versatile clothing that can be layered and adapted as needed.

**For Summer (May–October):**

- **Breathable Fabrics:** Bring plenty of lightweight, breathable clothing made from cotton, linen, or other airy materials. Items like sundresses, shorts, and tank tops are ideal for staying cool during the day.
- **Swimwear:** With pristine beaches and crystal-clear waters, don't forget your swimsuits, and consider a stylish sarong or beach cover-up for casual strolls along the shore or for boat trips.
- **Sun Protection:** A wide-brimmed hat and quality sunglasses are must-haves to shield you from the strong Mediterranean sun.
- **Footwear:** Given the steep, often cobbled streets of Amalfi's towns, pack comfortable walking shoes or sandals that combine support with style. Also, include a pair of slightly dressier shoes for evening outings.
- **Light Outerwear:** Although evenings are generally warm, a light jacket or sweater is advisable—especially in higher-altitude towns like Ravello—when the temperature drops or the sea breeze picks up.

**For Winter (November–April):**

- **Layered Clothing:** Winters here are relatively mild but can be damp, so bring layers such as long-sleeve shirts, light sweaters, and a versatile jacket.
- **Waterproof Outerwear:** Even though the region doesn't experience heavy rain, occasional showers are possible. Pack a water-resistant jacket or a compact umbrella to stay dry.
- **Appropriate Footwear:** Waterproof boots are essential if you plan to explore on foot during wetter weather or to traverse rugged terrain.

2. Footwear for Exploration

Since exploring the Amalfi Coast is best done on foot, selecting the right footwear is critical:

- **Hiking Shoes:** For adventures like the Path of the Gods, opt for lightweight, sturdy hiking shoes with excellent grip.
- **Water Shoes/Flip-Flops:** For beach days or visits to coastal caves like the Emerald Grotto, bring flip-flops or water shoes to protect your feet and enhance comfort.
- **Casual, Stylish Footwear:** For exploring charming coastal towns such as Positano, pack comfortable yet fashionable sandals or flats that work well for long walks and stylish outings.
- **Dress Shoes:** If you plan on enjoying fine dining at upscale restaurants, pack a pair of dress shoes or smart sandals to complement your formal attire.

3. Essential Accessories

Enhance your travel experience with these accessories that make every outing more convenient and enjoyable:

- **Beach Bag:** A spacious beach bag is essential for carrying all your seaside necessities—towels, sunscreen, snacks, and more—whether you're heading to the beach or boarding a boat.
- **Reusable Water Bottle:** Given the strong summer sun, staying hydrated is crucial. A refillable water bottle allows you to take advantage of free fresh spring water available in many towns.

- **Daypack:** For day trips and short hikes, a small backpack or crossbody bag is perfect for carrying essentials like your camera, wallet, and sunscreen.
- **Camera and Binoculars:** The Amalfi Coast is one of the world's most picturesque regions, so bring a camera (with extra batteries and memory cards) to capture every breathtaking view. Binoculars are also useful for spotting distant landmarks and enjoying nature's details.
- **Sunscreen and Lip Balm:** Protect your skin with a high-SPF sunscreen, and don't forget an SPF-infused lip balm for added defense against the sun's harsh rays.

4. Toiletries and Health Essentials

To maintain comfort and well-being throughout your journey:

- **Personal Toiletries:** Although most accommodations offer basic toiletries, it's wise to pack your own toothbrush, toothpaste, shampoo, conditioner, and body wash for added convenience.
- **First Aid Kit:** A compact first aid kit should include band-aids, antiseptic wipes, and pain relievers to handle minor scrapes or headaches.
- **Medications:** Ensure you bring enough of any prescription medications you need, and carry the original prescription documents for any potential refills.
- **Insect Repellent:** Especially in the warmer months, mosquitoes can be a nuisance. Pack insect repellent to keep bugs at bay during your outdoor excursions.

5. Travel Essentials

Stay organized and prepared with these must-have travel items:

- **Travel Documents:** Keep your passport, travel insurance, and printed confirmations for flights, hotels, and tours easily accessible. Consider making photocopies or digital backups for extra security.
- **Money and Payment Options:** While credit cards are widely accepted, having some cash in euros is beneficial in smaller towns or for street vendors.
- **Electronic Accessories:** Bring necessary chargers, a portable power bank, and a European power adapter (Italy uses Type F plugs with a

220V system) to keep your devices charged during long days of exploration.

## 6. Special Items for Luxury and Adventure Travelers

For those seeking a bit more indulgence or planning adventurous activities:

- **Formal Wear:** If you plan to dine at upscale restaurants or attend special events, pack elegant outfits such as a cocktail dress or a suit to complement your sophisticated surroundings.
- **Specialized Outdoor Gear:** For activities like hiking or boating, consider packing waterproof gear, a dry bag, or other specialized equipment to ensure a safe and comfortable experience.

## 7. What to Leave Behind

Avoid overpacking to ensure a hassle-free trip:

- **Excessive Luggage:** The best way to enjoy the Amalfi Coast is on foot, so pack light with a manageable suitcase or backpack to keep mobility high.
- **Valuable Jewelry:** It's advisable to leave expensive jewelry at home to avoid loss or damage, especially given the sandy beaches and busy tourist spots.

## Summary

This comprehensive packing guide for the Amalfi Coast covers all the essentials you need to fully immerse yourself in the region's enchanting beauty. By packing versatile clothing for varying weather conditions, appropriate footwear for both rugged trails and elegant evenings, and the right accessories and travel essentials, you'll be well-prepared for every adventure—from hiking breathtaking cliffside paths to savoring al fresco dinners by the sea. With smart preparation, you can ensure that your Amalfi Coast getaway is as comfortable as it is unforgettable, allowing you to relish every moment in one of Italy's most iconic destinations.

## 8.2 Budgeting & Cost-Saving Tips for the Amalfi Coast

The Amalfi Coast is one of Italy's most captivating destinations, celebrated for its dramatic cliffs, charming villages, and mesmerizing Mediterranean vistas. However, its allure often comes with a steep price tag—ranging from luxury accommodations to gourmet dining experiences. With careful planning and a few savvy strategies, you can immerse yourself in the beauty of the Amalfi Coast without overspending. Here are some detailed budgeting tips and cost-saving ideas to help you enjoy a memorable trip without breaking the bank.

1. Travel Timing: Choose the Off-Season

One of the most effective ways to trim your travel expenses is by avoiding the peak tourist months. While the summer season (June to September) offers ideal weather and bustling activity, it also brings higher prices for flights, hotels, and attractions.

- **When to Go:** The shoulder seasons—spring (April–May) and autumn (October–November)—provide pleasant weather, fewer crowds, and significantly lower prices.
- **Benefits:** Enjoy discounted airfare, lower accommodation rates, and potentially reduced prices for tours and activities. Additionally, experiencing the Amalfi Coast during these quieter periods means you can appreciate the region's natural beauty and cultural heritage without the overwhelming tourist rush.

2. Affordable Accommodation Options

Accommodation costs on the Amalfi Coast can vary dramatically depending on your chosen town and the level of luxury you desire.

- **Budget-Friendly Stays:** Look for modest guesthouses, B&Bs, or small motels in less-visited areas such as Minori, Maiori, or Praiano. Prices in these areas can be significantly lower than in hotspots like Positano or Amalfi.
- **Mid-Range Options:** Consider mid-range hotels or locally owned motels that offer comfortable amenities, such as complimentary

breakfast, free Wi-Fi, and pools, generally costing between €100 and €200 per night.
- **Luxury and Unique Stays:** If you're seeking a more indulgent experience, upscale resorts and boutique hotels provide exceptional service and breathtaking views, with prices ranging from €200 to €500 per night. For a truly distinctive experience, explore alternative options such as glamping sites, traditional adobe houses, or charming rural villas.
- **Tip:** Booking your accommodation well in advance and considering locations slightly away from the main tourist hubs can result in substantial savings.

3. Cost-Effective Transportation

Navigating the Amalfi Coast doesn't have to be expensive if you plan your transportation carefully.

- **Public Transportation:** Utilize the SITA bus network, which offers affordable rides between major towns like Positano, Amalfi, and Ravello for as little as €2–€5 per trip. Additionally, ferries are a scenic alternative to road travel, with fares typically ranging from €8 to €20.
- **Trains:** If you're arriving from further afield, consider taking a train to nearby cities such as Naples or Salerno, where you can connect to local buses or ferries.
- **Car Rentals:** Although renting a car offers flexibility, it can be challenging due to narrow roads and limited parking. If you opt to drive, consider renting a compact car for better fuel efficiency and easier maneuverability.
- **Pro Tip:** Look into multi-day transport passes or combined ticket packages that offer discounts for frequent use of buses or ferries.

4. Enjoy Free & Low-Cost Activities

The Amalfi Coast is rich in natural beauty and cultural history, and many experiences don't require a high price tag.

- **Beach Days:** Enjoy the coast's pristine beaches like Spiaggia Grande, Marina di Praia, and Minori Beach, which are free to access. While renting sunbeds or umbrellas might incur a small fee, simply lounging on the sand is an inexpensive pleasure.

- **Hiking and Walking Tours:** Explore the iconic Path of the Gods or wander through the narrow, scenic streets of the coastal villages. Many of these activities are completely free and offer a chance to soak in the stunning landscapes.
- **Local Attractions:** Visit historical churches, public squares, and markets that often offer free entry. A leisurely stroll through these cultural hubs is a fantastic way to experience local life without spending a lot.
- **Tip:** Research free entry days at museums and parks, which can help you plan your itinerary around cost-saving opportunities.

5. Smart Dining on a Budget

While fine dining is a hallmark of the Amalfi Coast, there are plenty of ways to enjoy delicious local cuisine without overspending.

- **Eat Where Locals Dine:** Venture away from the tourist-centric restaurants and try local trattorias and pizzerias in less crowded areas. These establishments often serve authentic Italian meals at a fraction of the price.
- **Street Food:** Savor iconic local street food such as frittura di pesce, sfogliatella, and pizza margherita from small stalls or markets, where prices can range from €5 to €8 per item.
- **Lunch Specials:** Many restaurants offer set lunch menus or specials during the day, providing excellent value compared to dinner prices.
- **Tip:** Avoid restaurants with multi-language menus and flashy displays, which are often designed to lure tourists and may charge premium prices.

6. Buy Local and Save

Supporting local artisans and businesses can be both economical and enriching.

- **Local Products:** Purchase limoncello, olive oil, handmade ceramics, and other artisanal products directly from local markets or small shops. These items are often more affordable and authentic than those found in tourist centers.

- **Pro Tip:** Hitting up local markets not only helps you save money but also gives you a deeper insight into the culture and traditions of the Amalfi Coast.

7. Take Advantage of Package Deals & Tours

Many tour operators and travel agencies offer bundled deals that combine several experiences, such as boat tours, guided hikes, and cultural excursions, at discounted rates.

- **Day Tours:** Look for group or half-day tours that include multiple attractions. These packages often cover transportation, guide fees, and entrance tickets, making them a cost-effective way to explore.
- **Group Discounts:** Consider joining group tours rather than booking private ones, as this can significantly reduce costs while still providing professional guidance and insight.
- **Pro Tip:** Check websites like Groupon or Travelzoo for special promotions and package deals that can further cut your expenses.

Summary

Traveling to the Amalfi Coast doesn't have to be an expensive affair. By planning ahead and utilizing these budgeting strategies, you can experience all the splendor of this Italian gem while keeping your expenses in check. Opting to travel during off-peak seasons, choosing budget-friendly accommodations, using public transportation, enjoying free or low-cost activities, and dining at local establishments are all excellent ways to stretch your budget. With thoughtful planning and savvy choices, you'll be able to savor every moment of your Amalfi Coast vacation, from its breathtaking views to its rich cultural experiences, without overspending.

## 8.3 Local Customs & Etiquette

Visiting the Amalfi Coast is not just about soaking in its scenic beauty, but also about understanding and respecting the local culture. Italians, particularly in smaller towns along the coast, take great pride in their traditions and way of life. Being aware of the local customs and etiquette can enhance your experience, help you avoid misunderstandings, and make your visit more enjoyable. Here are some essential **local customs and etiquette** to keep in mind while exploring this stunning region.

## 1. Greetings & Social Etiquette

In the Amalfi Coast, as in most of Italy, **greetings** play an important role in daily life, and locals appreciate when visitors make the effort to greet them properly.

**How to Greet People**

- **Formal Greetings**: Italians often greet each other with a handshake, particularly in more formal settings. For closer friends or family, **kisses on both cheeks** (starting with the left) are common. However, it's important to wait for the local to initiate the cheek-kissing, especially if you're not familiar with them.
- **Saying "Buongiorno" and "Buonasera"**: Use **"Buongiorno"** (Good morning) until around 2 PM and switch to **"Buonasera"** (Good evening) after that. A simple **"Ciao"** (Hello/Goodbye) is also widely accepted, but it's best used with friends or people you know well.
- **Polite Phrases**: It is always appreciated to say **"Per favore"** (Please) and **"Grazie"** (Thank you) in any interaction. A simple **"Scusi"** (Excuse me) goes a long way when trying to get someone's attention or ask for directions.

**Respect Personal Space**

- Italians value personal space, but it is often a bit closer than what might be typical in some other cultures. However, don't stand too close to someone unless you are in a casual or familiar setting. A bit of space is important, especially in formal contexts.

## 2. Dining Etiquette

Food is at the heart of life on the Amalfi Coast, and meals are an essential part of the daily rhythm. There are a few specific dining customs and expectations to keep in mind while enjoying the incredible cuisine of the region.

**When Dining Out**

- **Tipping**: Tipping is not as obligatory in Italy as it is in some countries, but it is still appreciated. In restaurants, you can leave a tip of around **5-10%** if the service is good. However, some restaurants may already include a **coperto** (a cover charge for bread and table service), which typically ranges from **€1 to €3** per person. If so, there is no need to tip extra for the service.
- **Punctuality**: Italians tend to eat dinner late, usually between **8 PM and 9 PM**, so if you're dining at a restaurant, plan accordingly. In more touristy areas, you may find places opening earlier, but for an authentic experience, aim for the later hours.
- **Courses**: Italian meals typically consist of several courses, often including an **antipasto** (appetizer), **primo** (first course, often pasta or soup), **secondo** (main course, usually meat or fish), and **contorno** (side dishes). You'll often see locals enjoying a leisurely meal, taking time between courses to savor each one.
- **Bread**: Italians love their bread, but remember that it's served for dipping or as part of the meal and shouldn't be eaten with butter or olive oil unless part of the custom. It's also polite to break the bread with your hands rather than cutting it.
- **Don't Rush**: Dining is a social activity, and meals are meant to be savored. Avoid rushing through your meal, and enjoy the conversation and leisurely pace of dining. Meals can last anywhere from **90 minutes to two hours**, depending on the course selection.

**3. Dress Code & Appearance**

Italians are known for their fashion sense, and the Amalfi Coast is no exception. Even in relaxed settings, people tend to dress with style and attention to detail. While there's no formal dress code for tourists, it's always a good idea to dress neatly and respectfully, especially in certain settings.

**What to Wear**

- **Casual Yet Stylish**: In the Amalfi Coast, it's important to maintain a balance between **casual and stylish**. In the daytime, lightweight,

breathable fabrics are ideal, especially if you're walking around the cliffs or visiting beaches. However, avoid wearing beachwear in towns or restaurants.
- **Evening Wear**: When dining out or attending an evening event, consider **smart casual** clothing. Men can wear a collared shirt and trousers, while women might choose a sundress or elegant top with pants or a skirt.
- **Footwear**: Comfortable shoes are essential if you plan on walking around the cliffs and hills. **Sturdy sandals or sneakers** are great for day trips, while more elegant shoes are suitable for dinners or visits to churches.

**Modesty in Churches**

- When visiting churches or religious sites, it is customary to dress modestly. **Covering your shoulders** and **wearing longer pants or skirts** is expected in places like the **Cathedral of Amalfi** or **Villa Rufolo**. Bring a scarf or shawl to cover your shoulders if needed.

## 4. Social & Cultural Norms

While the Amalfi Coast may seem laid-back, Italians take their social and cultural customs seriously. Here are a few things to keep in mind when interacting with locals.

**Respect for Family and Traditions**

- Italians value **family**, and family ties are very important. It's not uncommon for extended families to live close by and spend a lot of time together, especially during meals. Show respect for these family values, and you'll earn the locals' admiration.
- **Punctuality**: Italians are typically **relaxed** about punctuality in social settings, but for professional appointments, being on time is important. For social gatherings or casual outings, a few minutes of delay is often fine, but don't overstay your welcome.

**Noise Level**

- The Amalfi Coast is generally a **quiet** region, especially in the more remote towns. While it's fine to chat or laugh with friends in public spaces, try not to be overly loud, particularly in the evenings. Italians appreciate a more **calm and respectful atmosphere** in public places.

## 5. Public Behavior & Interaction

Understanding local manners and expectations can ensure you blend in harmoniously with locals.

### Public Transportation

- When traveling on buses or ferries, always be **polite** and respectful to others. Italians value personal space, but crowded conditions can sometimes make it impossible to avoid getting close to others. It's important to remain calm and patient, even during busy times.

### Interaction with Locals

- If you're looking for directions or advice, remember to always start with a **friendly greeting**. Italians are generally very helpful and willing to assist tourists, but it's important to be **respectful of their time**.
- **Don't Interrupt**: When engaging in conversation, especially in a group, avoid interrupting people. Italians are passionate talkers, but they respect the flow of conversation and waiting for your turn to speak.

Understanding and respecting the local **customs and etiquette** can make your visit to the Amalfi Coast not only more enjoyable but also a more enriching cultural experience. Whether you're savoring a leisurely meal, enjoying an afternoon espresso in a café, or exploring the quaint streets, remembering these social norms and practices will help you connect with the region's friendly locals while showing respect for its deep-rooted traditions. Buon viaggio!

# Chapter 9. Day Trips & Excursions

## 9.1 Pompeii & Mount Vesuvius: A Journey into the Past and the Power of Nature

Just a short drive from the Amalfi Coast, two of Italy's most iconic sites await—the ancient city of Pompeii and the mighty Mount Vesuvius. Together, these landmarks provide an extraordinary opportunity to step back into the world of ancient Rome and witness nature's formidable power.

Pompeii – A Glimpse into Ancient Roman Life

### A City Frozen in Time

Pompeii was once a thriving Roman city until the catastrophic eruption of Mount Vesuvius in 79 AD buried it under layers of ash and pumice. Its rediscovery in the 18th century offered historians and travelers a unique window into the past, preserving everyday life, architecture, and art from nearly two millennia ago. Walking through Pompeii's well-preserved streets, you can explore ancient homes, temples, public baths, and theaters, gaining an intimate understanding of Roman culture and society.

### Location & Details:

- **Address:** Pompeii Archaeological Site, Piazza Anfiteatro, 80045 Pompeii NA, Italy
- **GPS Coordinates:** 40.7494° N, 14.4843° E
- **Proximity:** Approximately 40 km from Amalfi—about a 1.5-hour drive.
- **Operating Hours:** Open daily from 9:00 AM to 7:00 PM (last entry at 5:30 PM); closed on December 25th.
- **Admission:** Standard ticket costs €15; reduced rate of €8 for EU citizens aged 18-24; free for children under 18, EU citizens with disabilities, and EU teachers.
- **Highlights:**
    - **The Forum:** The city's ancient civic center, once bustling with commerce and community life.
    - **The Amphitheater:** One of the world's best-preserved Roman amphitheaters, capable of seating 20,000 spectators.
    - **Villa of the Mysteries:** Renowned for its vivid frescoes that depict the Dionysian mysteries.

- **House of the Faun:** A grand residence famed for its intricate mosaics, including the celebrated Alexander Mosaic.
    - **Plaster Casts of Victims:** Chilling casts that capture the final moments of Pompeii's inhabitants, offering a poignant glimpse into the disaster.
- **Visitor Services:** Audio guides, guided tours, visitor centers, cafes, restrooms, and gift shops enhance your visit.

Mount Vesuvius – Nature's Fiery Sentinel

## An Active Volcano and a Living Laboratory

Mount Vesuvius, the volcano responsible for Pompeii's downfall, remains one of the most famous active volcanoes in the world. Standing at 1,281 meters (4,203 feet), Vesuvius dominates the Bay of Naples and offers dramatic, panoramic views of the surrounding landscape, including the Sorrentine Peninsula and the islands of Capri and Ischia. A hike to the crater provides not only a thrilling adventure but also a chance to learn about volcanic activity and the geological forces that continue to shape the region.

## Location & Details:

- **Address:** Parco Nazionale del Vesuvio, 80044 Ottaviano NA, Italy
- **GPS Coordinates:** 40.8224° N, 14.4280° E
- **Proximity:** Approximately 45 km from Amalfi, roughly a 1.5-hour drive.
- **Operating Hours:**
    - **April to October:** 9:00 AM – 6:00 PM
    - **November to March:** 9:00 AM – 3:00 PM
    - **Closed:** January 1st and December 25th
- **Admission:** General entry is €10; reduced rate of €5 for EU citizens aged 18-24; free for children under 18 and EU citizens with disabilities.
- **Highlights:**
    - **Crater Summit:** A challenging hike to the volcano's rim where you can peer into the vast crater and experience the raw power of volcanic forces.
    - **Panoramic Views:** The summit offers breathtaking vistas of the Bay of Naples, Pompeii, and the surrounding hills, making it a photographer's paradise.

- - **Volcanic Science Center:** Interactive exhibits at the visitor center provide insights into the eruption of 79 AD and ongoing monitoring of the volcano's activity.
- **Visitor Services:** Guided tours in multiple languages, shuttle buses from the base to the crater, parking facilities, restrooms, and a café.

Connecting the Past and the Present

A combined visit to Pompeii and Mount Vesuvius offers an unparalleled experience where you can explore the remnants of an ancient civilization and witness the enduring power of nature. Whether you opt to drive for the flexibility of stopping along scenic routes or take a guided tour that seamlessly connects the two sites, this day trip is both educational and awe-inspiring.

Why Visit?

Exploring Pompeii allows you to immerse yourself in the daily life of ancient Romans, providing a tangible connection to history through remarkably preserved ruins and artifacts. In contrast, hiking Mount Vesuvius offers a dramatic encounter with nature, letting you experience the dynamic forces that have shaped this part of Italy over centuries. Together, these sites encapsulate the essence of the Amalfi Coast—a place where history and natural beauty converge in an unforgettable landscape.

Conclusion

A trip to Pompeii and Mount Vesuvius is more than just a day out; it's a transformative journey that takes you from the quiet streets of an ancient city to the rugged, awe-inspiring slopes of a living volcano. Whether you are fascinated by history, intrigued by geological wonders, or simply seeking a profound adventure, this experience promises to leave an indelible mark on your memory. Explore, learn, and be inspired by the enduring legacy of these monumental sites on the Amalfi Coast.

## 9.2 Naples & Its Culinary Delights

Naples, the pulsating heart of the Campania region, is just a short drive from the Amalfi Coast and is a veritable feast for the senses—especially when it comes to food. Famed as the birthplace of pizza and celebrated for its bountiful seafood and exquisite pastries, Naples offers an immersive culinary journey that goes far beyond simple dining. A day trip to this bustling city is not only an opportunity to explore ancient streets and historic landmarks, but also a chance to savor time-honored recipes that embody the true spirit of Italian cuisine.

A Culinary Legend in Every Bite

Naples' gastronomic heritage is steeped in history, with every dish narrating a story of ancient traditions and locally sourced ingredients. The city's vibrant atmosphere is palpable from the moment you step onto its busy streets, where the aroma of freshly baked pizza, the sizzling sound of fried sfogliatella—a delicate, layered pastry—and the robust scent of rich espresso mingle in the air. Dining in Naples is not merely about eating; it's about experiencing the culture through its food. Whether you find yourself in a lively pizzeria, wandering through a bustling market, or sitting down in a family-owned trattoria, you're in for a culinary adventure that will linger in your memory.

Highlights of Naples' Culinary Scene

- Pizza Napoletana:
  Naples proudly claims the title of the birthplace of Pizza Margherita. Crafted with the finest tomatoes, fresh mozzarella, fragrant basil, and a drizzle of olive oil atop a perfectly chewy crust, this pizza is a simple yet divine expression of Italian culinary artistry. Legendary pizzerias such as Da Michele and Sorbillo have built their reputations on serving this iconic dish, drawing pizza enthusiasts from around the globe.

- Sfogliatella:
  No trip to Naples is complete without sampling sfogliatella—a pastry that's as much a work of art as it is a dessert. With its paper-thin layers of crispy dough enveloping a sweet, creamy ricotta filling, these seashell-shaped treats are best enjoyed warm, accompanied by a strong cup of espresso in the historic corridors of Spaccanapoli.

- Seafood Extravaganza:
  Thanks to its coastal location, Naples offers an unparalleled selection of seafood. Enjoy classics like spaghetti alle vongole, where succulent clams are paired with al dente pasta in a garlic-infused olive oil sauce, or try a mixed fried seafood platter known as frittura di paranza. For the freshest catch, the vibrant Fish Market at Piazza della Pignasecca is a must-visit, where local vendors serve up the ocean's bounty with authentic flair.

- Caffè Napoletano:
  For Neapolitans, coffee is an art form. The traditional Neapolitan espresso is renowned for its rich, robust flavor and is best experienced at historic cafés such as Gran Caffè Gambrinus. Here, you can enjoy a perfect pairing of caffè with a sweet pastry, a ritual that encapsulates the city's deep-rooted love for coffee.

- Limoncello:
  While often associated with the Amalfi Coast, limoncello is also a beloved treat in Naples. This vibrant, tangy lemon liqueur, made from locally grown lemons, is the perfect digestivo after a sumptuous meal. Numerous local shops and cafés offer their own versions of limoncello, each with its own distinctive twist.

Where to Dine in Naples
- Da Michele:
  Revered for its quintessential Pizza Margherita, Da Michele is a must-visit for pizza aficionados. Located on Via Cesare Sersale, this historic pizzeria continues to serve up simple yet extraordinary pies.

- Sorbillo:
  Another iconic pizzeria, Sorbillo on Via dei Tribunali, is famed for its soft-crust pizzas bursting with flavor—a true testament to the art of Neapolitan pizza-making.

- Gran Caffè Gambrinus:
  Step into this centuries-old café on Via Chiaia to experience the traditional Neapolitan coffee culture. Its elegant interiors and delightful pastries make it the perfect stop for a mid-morning or afternoon

break.

- Antica Trattoria da Nennella:
    For a more authentic taste of local life, visit this family-run trattoria located on Vico Lungo Teatro Nuovo, where you can sample hearty, traditional Neapolitan dishes in a casual, welcoming setting.

Getting There from the Amalfi Coast
Traveling from the Amalfi Coast to Naples is both convenient and scenic.
- By Car: Naples is approximately a 1-hour drive (about 60 km) from the Amalfi Coast, offering flexibility and the chance to enjoy coastal views along the way.
- By Train: The Circumvesuviana train from Sorrento to Naples takes roughly 1 hour and runs frequently, making it an efficient option.
- By Bus: SITA buses operate regularly from Amalfi and Positano to Naples, providing a cost-effective alternative.

Why Visit Naples?
Naples is not only the cradle of pizza but also a vibrant culinary epicenter that captures the heart and soul of Italian cuisine. The city's dynamic food scene reflects a rich tapestry of history and local traditions, offering an immersive experience that engages all your senses. For food lovers and culture enthusiasts alike, Naples promises an unforgettable journey through flavor, history, and the art of fine dining.

In summary, a visit to Naples is a deep dive into the culinary traditions that have shaped Italy's gastronomic reputation. Whether you're savoring a slice of authentic pizza, indulging in a sweet sfogliatella, or sampling freshly caught seafood, the city's vibrant food culture is an essential part of the Amalfi Coast experience.

## 9.3 Paestum & Ancient Greek Temples

For history buffs and those fascinated by ancient civilizations, a day trip to **Paestum**, located to the south of the Amalfi Coast, is a must. This UNESCO World Heritage site is home to some of the best-preserved **Greek temples** in the world, offering a glimpse into Italy's ancient past, long before the Romans made their mark on the peninsula.

## A Short Story

Paestum, once a Greek colony known as **Poseidonia**, dates back to the 6th century BC. Over time, it was overtaken by the Romans, but the site remained remarkably intact. The temples of Paestum stand as magnificent examples of Doric architecture, and their grandeur remains awe-inspiring even after more than 2,500 years. Today, visitors walk through the ruins of this ancient city, surrounded by fields of wildflowers and the distant sound of the waves crashing on the nearby coastline. Paestum is one of the most peaceful and awe-inspiring historical sites in Italy.

## Location:

- **Address**: Parco Archeologico di Paestum, 84047 Paestum SA, Italy
- **GPS Coordinates**: 40.4090° N, 15.0005° E
- **Distance from Amalfi Coast**: Approximately **1.5 hours** by car (about 105 km from Amalfi).

## Opening Hours:

- **Winter (November – March)**: **8:30 AM to 5:00 PM**
- **Summer (April – October)**: **8:30 AM to 7:30 PM**
- Closed on **December 25th**.

## Price:

- **General Admission**: €12
- **Reduced Price**: €6 (for EU citizens between 18-24 years old).
- **Free entry** for children under **18 years old**, EU citizens with disabilities, and teachers from the European Union.

## Website:

www.paestum.org

## Key Features:

1. **Temple of Hera**: The largest and most famous of the temples at Paestum, built in the 5th century BC.

2. **Temple of Neptune**: A beautifully preserved example of Doric architecture, often mistaken for the Temple of Poseidon.
3. **Temple of Ceres**: Smaller but still magnificent, showcasing Paestum's importance as a religious center.
4. **The Paestum Museum**: Housing artifacts from the archaeological site, including Greek pottery and ancient sculptures.
5. **The City Walls and Gates**: You can still walk along parts of the city's original walls, offering a unique perspective on the ancient settlement.

**Visitor Services:**

- **Guided Tours** are available for an extra fee.
- **Audio Guides** in multiple languages can be rented at the entrance.
- **Visitor Center** offers brochures, maps, and other resources.
- **Cafés** and **restaurants** near the site for lunch or snacks.
- **Restrooms** and a **gift shop**.

**How to Get There from the Amalfi Coast**

- **By Car**: From Amalfi, drive along the coast for about **1.5 hours** (105 km) to reach Paestum.
- **By Train**: Take a train from **Salerno** to **Paestum** (about 30 minutes).
- **By Bus**: SITA buses run from **Salerno** to **Paestum**, and the trip takes approximately **1 hour**.

**Why You Should Visit**

Paestum is a peaceful and atmospheric place, ideal for history lovers. Its remarkable Greek temples stand as some of the best-preserved structures from the ancient world, and a visit provides both a visual and educational experience. For anyone interested in Greek history or architecture, Paestum is an essential stop that contrasts the vibrant tourist hotspots of the Amalfi Coast with a deeper look into Italy's ancient heritage.

# Chapter 10. Practical Information

Embarking on a journey to the Amalfi Coast offers an opportunity to immerse yourself in stunning landscapes, rich cultural heritage, and delectable cuisine. To ensure a seamless and enjoyable experience, it's essential to be well-prepared. This comprehensive guide provides crucial safety and health insights, along with practical advice on managing currency, accessing ATMs, and handling payments, empowering you to explore the Amalfi Coast with confidence.

## 10.1 Safety & Health Tips

While the Amalfi Coast is renowned for its safety, exercising standard precautions is advisable to ensure a worry-free trip. Whether you're wandering through cliffside villages, taking a dip in the Mediterranean, or trekking scenic trails, being mindful of safety considerations enhances your overall experience.

General Safety Tips
- Stay Confident: Adopt a confident demeanor while exploring to deter potential pickpockets.

- Transportation Choices: The Amalfi Coast's narrow, winding roads can be challenging for drivers unfamiliar with the terrain. Opting for ferries or hiring local drivers is recommended over self-driving.

- Health Coverage: Secure comprehensive travel health insurance that encompasses medical emergencies and accidents. While Italy boasts quality healthcare, having insurance ensures access to necessary medical attention without financial strain.

- Emergency Contacts: Familiarize yourself with Italy's emergency number, 112, which connects you to police, fire, and ambulance services. Keep your accommodation's contact information and the nearest embassy or consulate details handy.

- Sun Protection: With its sunny climate, the Amalfi Coast necessitates proper sun protection. Apply high-SPF sunscreen, wear a hat, and stay hydrated to prevent heat-related ailments, especially during summer.

- Water Safety: Before swimming, check local weather conditions and be aware of potential hazards like strong currents or jellyfish. Many beaches are rocky; wearing water shoes can provide added comfort and safety.

- Food and Water: Tap water in Italy is generally safe to drink. However, if you have a sensitive stomach, opt for bottled water. Be cautious when consuming street food—ensure it's fresh and prepared under hygienic conditions.

Health Care on the Amalfi Coast
- Pharmacies: Accessible in towns such as Positano, Amalfi, and Ravello, pharmacies offer a range of medications, including over-the-counter remedies, and can provide advice for common ailments.

- Medical Facilities: For serious health concerns, the Ospedale Santa Maria della Misericordia in Ravello serves as a nearby hospital. Various clinics along the coast cater to minor medical issues. Always carry your travel insurance details, as some treatments may require upfront payment.

- Vaccinations: No special vaccinations are required for travel to the Amalfi Coast. Nonetheless, consulting your doctor before traveling is advisable to ensure you're up-to-date with routine immunizations and to discuss any recommended vaccines based on your health history.

Currency, ATMs, and Payments
- Currency: Italy uses the Euro (€). It's advisable to carry some cash, as smaller establishments may prefer cash payments.

- ATMs: Widely available in towns along the Amalfi Coast, ATMs (known locally as 'Bancomat') allow you to withdraw cash using international debit or credit cards. Be aware of potential foreign transaction fees imposed by your home bank.

- Card Payments: Major credit and debit cards are accepted in most hotels, restaurants, and shops. However, some smaller businesses may only accept cash, so it's prudent to confirm payment methods beforehand.

- Tipping: Tipping is appreciated but not obligatory in Italy. In restaurants, a service charge ('coperto') is often included in the bill. If not, leaving a 10% tip is customary for good service.

By adhering to these guidelines and staying informed, you can fully embrace the enchanting allure of the Amalfi Coast, ensuring a memorable and secure journey.
1.

## 10.2 Currency, ATMs, and Payment Tips for the Amalfi Coast

Traveling along the Amalfi Coast means managing your money wisely to fully enjoy this stunning region without financial hassles. Since Italy uses the Euro (€), understanding the local payment landscape—from exchanging money and withdrawing cash to using credit cards and mobile payments—will ensure a smooth financial experience during your trip.

Currency and Exchange

**Currency Basics:**
 On the Amalfi Coast, the Euro is the currency used in every town, from the vibrant streets of Positano and Ravello to the historic center of Amalfi. Because exchange rates can fluctuate, it's a good idea to monitor them before you depart.

**Exchanging Money:**
 You have several options when it comes to obtaining Euros. Currency exchange services are available at major transit hubs such as airports and train stations, as well as in larger coastal towns. However, these exchange counters often offer less favorable rates and may charge additional commissions. For a better deal, consider withdrawing cash directly from ATMs.

**Exchange Offices:**
In towns like Sorrento and Amalfi, you'll find dedicated currency exchange offices. While these can be convenient, it's usually best to exchange only a small amount if needed and rely on ATMs for larger withdrawals.

ATMs

**Availability:**
ATMs are widely accessible along the Amalfi Coast, especially in well-populated areas like Positano, Amalfi, and Ravello, as well as in many smaller villages. However, if you plan to venture into more remote areas, it's wise to withdraw extra cash beforehand, as ATMs might be scarce.

**Fees and Limits:**
Keep in mind that your home bank may impose fees for international ATM withdrawals. To reduce these extra costs, try to withdraw larger sums at once while still staying within safe limits. Also, be aware that some ATMs have daily withdrawal limits, so plan your cash needs accordingly if you'll be out exploring for several days.

Card Payments and Mobile Options

**Credit and Debit Cards:**
Most hotels, upscale restaurants, and larger shops on the Amalfi Coast accept major credit and debit cards—Visa, Mastercard, and American Express are widely recognized. However, smaller establishments, local markets, and street vendors may operate on a cash-only basis, so it's wise to have some cash on hand for those instances.

**Mobile Payments:**
Modern payment methods like Apple Pay and Google Pay are increasingly accepted in more tech-savvy venues, though these options might not be available everywhere. Always have a backup form of payment, particularly in rural or less-developed areas.

Tipping and Local Practices

**Tipping Etiquette:**
Tipping in Italy is generally appreciated, even if not strictly expected. In restaurants, if a service charge isn't already included in your bill, a tip of

about 5–10% is customary for good service. For small services—such as taxis or porters—rounding up the fare is a common courtesy.

Tips for Handling Local Currency

**In Smaller Towns and Rural Areas:**
In less touristy spots along the Amalfi Coast, many businesses may only accept cash. Ensure you have a sufficient amount of small denomination Euros for purchases at local markets, street vendors, and small cafes.

**At Markets and Street Vendors:**
While larger stores and restaurants typically accept card payments, local vendors often deal exclusively in cash. Keeping an adequate supply of cash makes it easier to enjoy spontaneous finds and authentic local treats without any hassle.

Summary

- **Currency:** Italy's official currency is the Euro (€).
- **ATMs:** Readily available in major towns, but plan ahead if traveling to remote areas; be mindful of potential fees and withdrawal limits.
- **Payments:** Credit and debit cards are widely accepted in cities and tourist centers, but always carry cash for small businesses and rural markets.
- **Tipping:** Although not mandatory, leaving a 5–10% tip in restaurants is customary, and small tips for taxis and porters are appreciated.
- **Preparation:** Monitor exchange rates, use ATMs wisely, and have backup payment options for a hassle-free experience.

By following these practical tips and managing your finances effectively, you'll be well-equipped to explore the Amalfi Coast with confidence. Enjoy the breathtaking scenery, rich culture, and world-class cuisine knowing that your money matters are taken care of.

## 10.3 Language & Communication

The official language of Italy, including the Amalfi Coast, is **Italian**. While many people in tourist areas speak some level of English, learning a few basic phrases in Italian can enhance your experience and show respect for the local culture. Here's everything you need to know about language and communication on the Amalfi Coast.

**Common Phrases in Italian**

1. **Hello** – *Ciao* (informal), *Salve* (formal)
2. **Goodbye** – *Arrivederci*
3. **Please** – *Per favore*
4. **Thank you** – *Grazie*
5. **Yes** – *Sì*
6. **No** – *No*
7. **Excuse me** – *Mi scusi*
8. **How much does this cost?** – *Quanto costa questo?*
9. **Do you speak English?** – *Parli inglese?*
10. **Where is the bathroom?** – *Dove è il bagno?*

Learning a few basic words and phrases will not only help you navigate the Amalfi Coast but will also endear you to the locals. Many Italian people are proud of their language and appreciate when visitors make an effort to communicate in Italian.

**English in the Amalfi Coast**

In popular tourist towns like **Positano**, **Amalfi**, and **Sorrento**, many locals, especially those working in hospitality and restaurants, speak English to some degree. In rural areas, English may not be as widely spoken, so learning a few key phrases can be helpful. Don't be discouraged if someone doesn't speak fluent English—they will often do their best to assist you, and a friendly attitude goes a long way.

**Using Mobile Phones & Internet**

1. **SIM Cards**: If you're traveling from abroad, it's often cheaper to buy a local **Italian SIM card**. Major mobile networks like **TIM**, **Vodafone**, and **Wind** offer prepaid SIM cards, which can be found at airports, train stations, or local shops. This can be a more affordable option than international roaming plans.
2. **Wi-Fi**: Many hotels, cafes, and restaurants along the Amalfi Coast offer free Wi-Fi. However, the signal may not always be as strong in

more remote areas. For consistent internet access, especially for mapping and navigation, it's recommended to have a local SIM card with data.

**Emergency Services & Communication**

- **Emergency number in Italy**: **112** (for police, fire, and ambulance)
- **Tourist Information**: Most towns along the Amalfi Coast have tourist information centers that can provide help with directions, booking tours, and general queries. In major towns like Amalfi and Sorrento, these centers usually have English-speaking staff.
- **Hotel Reception**: Most hotels on the Amalfi Coast have English-speaking staff who can assist with reservations, transportation, and local information.

## 10.4 Sustainable & Responsible Travel

Sustainable travel is increasingly important, and the Amalfi Coast is no exception. As one of Italy's most beloved destinations, the region is under pressure from mass tourism. However, by making conscious choices, visitors can help preserve the natural beauty and cultural heritage of this stunning coastline. Here are some ways to travel responsibly on the Amalfi Coast.

**1. Respect for Nature**

- **Preserving Natural Beauty**: The Amalfi Coast is a UNESCO World Heritage site due to its breathtaking landscapes. When visiting natural attractions like the **Path of the Gods** or **Fiordo di Furore**, ensure that you leave no trace—take your litter with you and avoid disturbing wildlife.
- **Beach Conservation**: Many of the Amalfi Coast's beaches are rocky and secluded, with fragile ecosystems. Respect posted signs regarding swimming zones and avoid walking through delicate vegetation or disturbing marine life.
- **Sustainable Hiking**: When hiking in areas like **Ferriere Valley Nature Reserve**, stick to established trails to protect the flora and fauna. Avoid leaving markings or signs of your presence in nature, and respect any local rules or guidelines regarding trail use.

**2. Reducing Plastic Use**

Plastic pollution is a growing concern, particularly in popular coastal areas. Bring reusable water bottles, shopping bags, and containers for food and snacks. Many local shops and cafes along the Amalfi Coast have switched to offering alternatives to single-use plastics, and more eco-friendly businesses are gaining momentum.

- **Reusable Water Bottles**: In addition to helping reduce waste, bringing your own water bottle can help save money, as many towns now offer refill stations.
- **Shopping Bags**: While some shops provide biodegradable bags, it's still advisable to bring your own reusable cloth bag when shopping.

**3. Supporting Local Businesses**

- **Buy Local**: Shop at local markets and support artisans who create handmade products. From ceramics in Ravello to limoncello in Amalfi, buying locally supports the economy and helps preserve traditional crafts and trades.
- **Sustainable Restaurants**: Look for restaurants and cafes that use local, seasonal ingredients. Many eateries on the Amalfi Coast pride themselves on sourcing food from local farms and fishermen, reducing their environmental impact.
- **Farm-to-Table Dining**: Seek out restaurants that prioritize sustainable farming practices and local produce. The Amalfi Coast is known for its incredible citrus fruits, fresh seafood, and organic vegetables, which are often featured in farm-to-table meals.

**4. Eco-Friendly Transportation**

- **Use Public Transport**: Consider using local buses, ferries, and trains to get around, rather than relying on private car rentals. These forms of transportation are more eco-friendly and help reduce traffic congestion along the narrow roads of the Amalfi Coast.
- **Electric Scooters & Bikes**: Some towns, such as Sorrento, offer electric scooters and bicycles for rent, which are a great way to explore the coast without emitting harmful emissions.
- **Walking & Hiking**: Many of the Amalfi Coast's towns and villages are best explored on foot. Not only is this environmentally friendly, but it also allows you to enjoy the stunning views and charming streets at your own pace.

## 5. Cultural Sensitivity & Ethical Tourism

- **Respect Local Culture**: The Amalfi Coast has a rich cultural heritage, and it's important to respect local customs, traditions, and beliefs. Be polite, dress modestly when visiting churches or religious sites, and always ask before taking photographs of locals.
- **Avoid Overcrowding**: To avoid contributing to over-tourism, visit the Amalfi Coast in the shoulder seasons (spring or autumn) when the crowds are thinner and the weather is still pleasant.
- **Sustainable Souvenirs**: Choose souvenirs that are made locally and ethically, such as hand-painted ceramics or locally produced limoncello. Avoid mass-produced, non-sustainable items that might be harmful to the environment.

**Summary**

- **Learn Key Phrases**: While English is widely spoken, learning a few basic Italian phrases can enhance your experience and help you connect with locals.
- **Respect the Environment**: Minimize waste, avoid disrupting local wildlife, and take steps to preserve the natural beauty of the Amalfi Coast.
- **Support Sustainable Businesses**: Shop at local markets, dine at eco-friendly restaurants, and choose sustainable forms of transportation.
- **Be Culturally Sensitive**: Respect local traditions and customs, and practice responsible tourism by avoiding overcrowded spots and supporting ethical businesses.

By adopting sustainable and responsible travel practices, you contribute to the preservation of the Amalfi Coast for future generations, ensuring that its natural beauty and cultural heritage continue to thrive.

Printed in Dunstable, United Kingdom